the Godless delusion

the Godless delusion

A Catholic Challenge to Modern Atheism

Patrick Madrid and Kenneth Hensley

Our Sunday Visitor Publishing Division
Our Sunday Visitor, Inc.
Huntington, Indiana 46750

CONTENTS

INTRODUCTION

My first discussion about God with an atheist took place in 1971. I was a precocious eleven-year-old, and the atheist, a thirty-ish housewife who lived across the street, happened to be driving my sister and me somewhere as a favor to my mom. Sometime during that otherwise innocuous conversation, I mentioned God.

"God?" She gave a snort. "You believe in God, huh?"

"Yes . . ." I said timidly, confused by the sharp note of derision that so suddenly had entered her voice.

"Well, there's no such thing as God," she snapped. "He doesn't exist, and people who believe in God believe in a myth."

My heart started pounding. As a rather sheltered Catholic kid, I had never heard anything like that before. But being a plucky lad, seeing the irritation on her face in the rearview mirror goaded me to push back. And that's when I discovered I had nothing to push back with.

Atheist Lady sliced and diced my clumsy attempts to defend my childlike belief in God — a belief which, to her, was child*ish*. I couldn't answer her arguments, so I sat in embarrassed silence for the rest of the ride. Thus ended my earliest foray into the world of atheism.

Perhaps because I was so thoroughly routed, that encounter made an impression on me.

In the nearly forty years since that day, I've discovered the fatal flaws of atheism. Ah, if only I could go back in time! Knowing what I know now, were I to have another conversation with Atheist Lady, I believe things would play out rather differently.

At one time or another, most Catholics will be hassled by an atheist over their belief in God, even if only indirectly. Not everyone knows an atheist personally, but we all inhabit a society overrun with atheist proselytism. Anti-God propaganda forces its way into the public consciousness via the Internet, movies, billboards, and a recent avalanche of bellicose books, such as Christopher Hitchens' *God Is Not Great* and Richard Dawkins' *The God Delusion*.

This is a serious problem, to be sure — but one susceptible to a particular, highly effective solution, which we present in this book.

It has been an honor for me to co-author *The Godless Delusion* with my friend Kenneth Hensley. This collaboration is the result of our combined years of learning (often acquired in the School of Hard Knocks) and practical experience in dealing with atheists. We have pondered both the philosophical and cosmological reasons for believing in God, as well as the various atheist arguments against God. We've also studied atheists themselves — observing what they say and how they act.

The more we studied and discussed and observed atheism and atheists, the more convinced Kenneth and I became that the most effective way to debunk their arguments against God is through a thoroughgoing appeal to reason. True, our faith in God is vitally important to us as Catholics, but such faith does not impress atheists, who pride themselves as seeking truth solely on the basis of evidence, not "faith." Fair enough.

We believe in God not as a mere theoretical concept or because believing provides a comforting alternative to the bleak meaninglessness of atheism. Rather, we contend, there are solid, compelling reasons for believing, including our central premise of this book: that atheism, which is the sole alternative to the existence of God (i.e., he either exists or he doesn't), is itself utterly, irretrievably unreasonable.

"God?" Atheists ask. "You believe in *God*?"

Yes. We do.

Turn the page and we'll show you why. We'll demonstrate that only God's existence can provide a rational account for reality as we know it and, therefore, why the atheist alternative is just a delusion.

— Patrick Madrid

CHAPTER ONE

A TALE OF TWO WORLDVIEWS

In our great universities, naturalism — the doctrine that nature is "all there is" — is the virtually unquestioned assumption that underlies not only the natural sciences, but intellectual work of all kinds.

— Philip Johnson

THE NEW ATHEISM

Something strange and unsettling is happening in America. A fiercely militant, hegemonic, openly aggressive kind of godlessness is on the rise in the very country renowned the world over for its official motto, "In God We Trust."[1] A vociferous and hostile denial of God's existence is spreading steadily across this historically God-fearing nation, a nation our fathers brought forth on this continent more than 230 years ago with a Declaration of Independence that includes this solemn proclamation of belief in God:

> We hold these truths to be self-evident, that all men are created equal, that they are endowed by their Creator with certain unalienable Rights, that among these are Life, Liberty and the pursuit of Happiness. . . . appealing to the Supreme Judge of the world for the rectitude of our intentions . . . with a firm reliance on the protection of Divine Providence, we mutually pledge to each other our Lives, our Fortunes, and our sacred Honor.

The rising tide of militant atheism is sweeping rapidly across not just the United States but the West as a whole, swamping Western culture in the noxious morass of a worldview that regards belief in God as a prime enemy to be ruthlessly eradicated, wherever it may be found.

> The denial that God exists has been around for a very long time.

Atheism, of course, is nothing new. The denial that God exists has been around for a very long time. Fortunately, the number of "God-deniers" has historically been quite small when compared to the far larger number of people who believe in God — whether or not they live according to that belief. Lately, though — certainly within the last 150 years, and especially within the last 10 years — atheism has been gaining strength in numbers and outspokenness.

Many modern atheists are no longer content to take the "live-and-let-live" approach toward those who believe in God. They no longer seem content to simply sneer at theists, pitying them for such backward, anti-scientific superstition, and just leave them alone. Lately, in increasing numbers, atheists are becoming militant in their efforts to dissuade anyone who will listen from believing in God. They hate the idea of God, and thus, they hate the idea that some people would believe in Him. These atheists have been cranking out a steady stream of anti-God books, such as *Why I Am Not a Christian* (Bertrand Russell), *The God Delusion* (Richard Dawkins), *Breaking the Spell: Religion as a Natural Phenomenon* (Daniel Dennett), and *God Is Not Great* (Christopher Hitchens).[2] Following in the wake of these books are videos, television programs, magazine articles, lectures, and even urban billboard campaigns spreading the same message. Atheists are bent not simply on "proving," once and for all, that God does not exist, but on convincing believers to stop believing. They want more atheists to join them in the "fold."

A Threat to Society

Unfortunately, most Christians have been caught completely off-guard, flatfooted, and therefore woefully unprepared to counter this atheist onslaught. Some Christians who have, at best, a tenuous intellectual understanding of the reasons why they believe in God become rattled and worried by atheist arguments. Some lose their faith in God altogether as a result.

Consider the prevailing trends regarding belief in God that are at work in the West right now. Surveys[3] show that the vast majority of Americans believe in the existence of a personal God. Even so, the number of those who would refer to themselves as either agnostic ("I *don't know* whether God exists or not") or as atheist ("I *deny* God's existence") is not insubstantial — it's something in the vicinity of ten percent. This means that out of a total population of some 300 million Americans, *30 million* citizens doubt, or outright deny, the existence of God. That's a significant number of people who — if they were to operate as a group in a way consistent with their naturalistic worldview — would be in a position to do terrible damage to society.

If you're wondering right now whether that last statement might be a bit "over the top," please read on with an open mind. We will endeavor to make the case beyond a reasonable doubt that, if the atheist worldview were to be implemented across the board as the basis of social policy (as it *has* been, in limited fashion, at times in the twentieth century — with disastrous results), you would definitely not want to live in such a society, so brutal, tyrannical, and devoid of genuine goodness and beauty would it be. In subsequent chapters, we will explain why that is true.

For the moment, though, it's enough of a headache to simply ponder the fact that the West has, for some time now, been sliding steadily down the escarpment of the Culture of Doubt toward the precipice of atheism, beyond which lies only the abyss of godlessness and all the horrors contained within it. Just consider notable modern mass-murdering atheists such as Stalin, Mao, Planned Parenthood, and Pol Pot (and some heavily influenced by atheism, such as Hitler). Worse yet, there are fewer and fewer "speed bumps" in our culture formidable enough to slow this descent into darkness.

> Christians *must* begin taking the challenge of atheism seriously and learn how to effectively evangelize our increasingly atheistic culture.

This is why Christians *must* wake up to the crisis of godlessness. They *must* begin taking the challenge of atheism seriously and learn how to effectively evangelize our increasingly atheistic culture. Given the West's steadily-growing acceptance of the notion that science and technology — not God — are the real answers to society's many problems, it's more imperative now than ever that Christians understand how to answer atheism and defend the truth of the Christian theistic worldview.

ATHEISTS ON THE OFFENSIVE

Although the number of those who refer to themselves as either agnostic or atheist is somewhere around ten percent of the population, those who identify themselves as "*committed* philosophical atheists" are a much smaller number — about half of all professing atheists. That's the good news.

The bad news is that many of those who identify themselves as "committed" atheists, strongly devoted to proselytizing others, work within the academic and educational spheres. This gives them a disproportionately large influence on society, primarily from the scientific community and academia. Through the collective force of their published works, lectures, and classroom teaching, these atheists have a platform from which to advocate their beliefs and dictate the parameters of the groupthink that so often prevails in our venerable educational and cultural institutions.

Remarkably, this relatively small number of atheists has managed to cast a very broad net of doubt regarding belief in God. Among those working in academia in general, the percentage who say they either doubt or deny the real existence of a personal God — a God who created, cares about, and interacts with the world — runs somewhat higher than the national average. However, in the case of those engaged in the natural sciences in particular, the percentage rises dramatically. One study put the number at 60 percent; another, surveying only members of the National Academy of Sciences, indicated a possible figure as high as 93 percent. *Ninety-three percent* of a given population doubts or denies God's existence.[4]

Some of these people, then, establish the essential "view of things" that is presented as true and factual in our institutions of learning, both here in America and throughout the post-Christian West.

And they do so with gusto. From kindergarten through university, in textbooks, teaching, research, museums, magazines, scientific programming for television, and other media — everywhere — these atheists espouse the naturalist worldview with religious fervor. They present it with an "everyone knows" self-confidence that doesn't even require rational justification or proof. As a result of the highly successful campaign to inject the self-hardening epoxy of naturalism into every facet of the broader world of academia and the scientific community, this essentially atheist view of the universe has not just given the previously dominant theistic worldview "a run for its money." It has decisively supplanted theism at all levels and has emerged *de facto* as the officially accepted worldview. Naturalism is now very widely regarded as the simple, self-evident truth of how things are.

In his book *Reason in the Balance*, Christian apologist Philip Johnson describes the current situation in the academic establishment:

> The most influential intellectuals in America and around the world are mostly naturalists, who assume that God exists only as an idea in the minds of religious believers. In our great universities,

naturalism — the doctrine that nature is "all there is" — is the virtually unquestioned assumption that underlies not only the natural sciences, but intellectual work of all kinds.[5]

The sobering result is that — although most Americans believe in God — most American children, youth, and young adults are being systematically indoctrinated in the naturalist worldview by this dedicated minority. The social, moral, and political implications of this arrangement are ominous.

> Although most Americans believe in God, most American children, youth, and young adults are being systematically indoctrinated in the naturalist worldview.

The well-known twentieth-century philosopher Mortimer Adler once described the halls of academia as being "like the halls of a madhouse at midnight." But even in a madhouse, a certain insane view of "how things are in the real world" is communicated from inmate to inmate; a certain twisted orthodoxy is maintained. Likewise in academia. As students sit in lecture halls and walk along hallways, the "unquestioned assumptions" of their instructors are communicated, imbibed, absorbed. No clear and convincing arguments are made for the reigning naturalist-atheist orthodoxy — this is precisely the nature of *unquestioned* assumptions. That God does not exist is simply presupposed. It is continually implied, insinuated, suggested, understood, and *known* that, of course, naturalism is true and, therefore, there is no God.

Now, take the influence of an implicit and sometimes explicit naturalism in our educational system (implicit for children under twelve, explicit for everyone else). Add to this the confirming message of a secular popular culture, as communicated in TV, movies, music, and literature: "God's existence is, at best, irrelevant." Stir into this toxic brew an epidemic shattering of families and all that follows in terms of the inevitable confusion, anger, and distrust. It's no wonder that, especially among the young, the number of those who question the existence of God continues to increase.

Maybe there's a God, many people think to themselves, *but who knows for sure, and what does it matter anyway? No one can really know whether there's a God up there, so why bother with it?* And so, having been conditioned to think along these lines, fathers and mothers pass an incipient attitude of doubt and indifference to their children. Teachers pass it on to their students. The shadow of doubt lengthens, with the tragic result that those who are the very image and likeness of the God who loves them come to say within their hearts, "There is no God."

This is where things stand at present. But how did we get here?

LIFE STORIES

Let's begin by talking about stories and those who tell them. In one of the greatest essays ever written, *The Ethics of Elfland*, G.K. Chesterton writes, "I had always felt life first as a story — and if there is a story there is a story teller."[6]

It's so true. We *do* feel life first as a story. Each of us experiences his or her life as a *story*, as a grand drama unfolding before our eyes, with ourselves cast in the leading role. We don't know what is going to happen or where the story leads. Tomorrow will be another scene in the drama, another page in the story.

In this story — the drama of our lives — exist all the elements one would expect to find in any good novel. There is adventure, excitement, success, and failure. There is love and romance. There is

> Each day, we rise and enter into the story with no idea what the next turn in the plot line will be.

suffering, tragedy, and loss. There is suspense, surprise, mystery, and magic. Each day, we rise and enter into the story with no idea what the next turn in the plot line will be, or when and how it will come.

This is also how we share the details of our lives with others. Consider, for example, what you do when you meet someone you don't really want to get to know and whom you don't really want to get to know you. You keep the conversation light and abstract. "Pretty nice weather today, eh?" "Did you catch the big game on TV yesterday?" and so on. In contrast, when we *want* someone to know us, and want to know that someone, we do something very different — we share our stories.

And the more we desire to know and be known by another, the more of the story we want to hear and to tell. "Where were you born? When? Tell me about your family. What were your parents like? Any brothers and sisters? What was it like to grow up in a small town? When did you begin to love music? Tell me about your first love."

Instinctively we want to hear the whole story. And why? Because our stories communicate where we've come from, who we are, and who we're becoming, and as such they provide the context in which we can understand one another.

Because of this, the best and most satisfying stories are the ones that begin, naturally enough, at the beginning.

> To begin my life with the beginning of my life, I record that I was born (as I have been informed and believe) on a Friday, at twelve o'clock at night. It was remarked that the clock began to strike, and I began to cry, simultaneously.

That's how Charles Dickens began *David Copperfield*, a classic tale that has captivated readers' imaginations the world over. Dickens understood that the sweeping narrative of his character's life would be best understood by beginning at the beginning and telling the entire story. Similarly, the Catholic mystic Thomas Merton began his autobiographical work, *The Seven Storey Mountain*, along similar lines:

> On the last day of January 1915, under the sign of the Water Bearer, in a year of a great war, and down in the shadow of some French mountains near the border of Spain, I came into the world.

There's a feeling of satisfaction we experience when we read the first lines of these stories. A feeling of, "Okay, this is going to be good." After all, if we're going to read the life of a person, to really hear their story, we want to hear it from the beginning. We understand intuitively that for the details to make sense, we have to see them within the context of the entire story.

CREATION STORIES

Now let's take a step back to consider the larger "stories" that make sense of *our* stories. As exciting and meaningful as our individual stories may be, as crucial for understanding who we are, our stories — yours and mine — still leave the most important questions about *our lives* unanswered:

- Why am I here?
- What is the ultimate purpose of my life?
- Beyond family and friends and occupation and personal interests, is there something I've been created for?
- *Have* I been created?
- Where *have* I come from, ultimately — and where, ultimately, am I going?
- What is the big picture, and how should I live in the light of that big picture?

In order to get answers to these larger questions — answers, by the way, that are *required* if we are to make sense of our individual stories and not experience them as a mere series of events — a *larger story needs to be told.*

What is needed is some *macro* story that can provide a context for and make sense of the *micro* stories of our individual lives. We all instinctively want to know how the individual "subplot" of our lives fits into the Big Story.

Every human being wonders about these things and asks these same questions, and civilizations and societies *always do have* some answer. This answer, not surprisingly, comes in the form of a story itself — a tale told, and believed, that provides "the rest of the story" for that civilization. Phillip Johnson refers to these as civilization's "creation stories" because these stories answer the questions about where the world came from, where we came from, and what the purpose of life is. These stories provide the context in which the life of a civilization or society can be rendered meaningful.

THE CHRISTIAN STORY

For more than 1,700 years, the story that was told and believed throughout the far-flung reaches of what we call Western Civilization was the Judeo-Christian theistic story. In other words, the vast majority of people lived out the stories of their lives, individually and collectively, with a conscious realization that God does indeed exist. For the Jews, the opening lines of the story began:

> In the beginning, God created the heavens and the earth.

Once Jesus Christ, the Messiah and Redeemer, burst onto the stage of human events, forever changing and elevating the course of the story, a Christian eyewitness to that new chapter began his narration this way:

> In the beginning was the Word, and the Word was with God, and the Word was God. . . .And the Word became flesh and dwelt among us.

During the past 2,000 years or so, most people in the West understood, even if only implicitly, that the drama

During the past 2,000 years or so, most people in the West understood that the drama of their own lives was inextricably bound up within the grand cosmic drama of creation.

of their own lives was inextricably bound up within the grand cosmic drama of creation. They knew that they had been brought into existence by a personal God. They understood intuitively that, without acknowledging the Big Story, no one's individual story would have any meaning. This intuition is as true today for us as it was back then for them.

Of course, our use of the word "story" isn't saying that it wasn't true; this story was, and is, certainly true. But nevertheless, like our lives, it came to us as a story. And like all great stories, this story began at the very beginning: "In the beginning God created the heavens and the earth..." (Gen 1:1).

The essential lines of what we will refer to as the Christian theistic story[7] are well known. An infinite personal God exists and created all things. We are not merely bodies but embodied souls, spirits made in God's very image and likeness, to be His sons and daughters, intended to share eternally in all that He possesses. As God's children, we have meaning and purpose that extend far beyond the few years we may have in this world. While here, we must live in our Father's love and in accordance with the moral laws He has written on our very hearts and revealed to us through his Son, Jesus Christ.

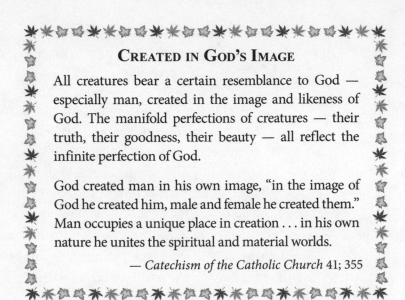

CREATED IN GOD'S IMAGE

All creatures bear a certain resemblance to God — especially man, created in the image and likeness of God. The manifold perfections of creatures — their truth, their goodness, their beauty — all reflect the infinite perfection of God.

God created man in his own image, "in the image of God he created him, male and female he created them." Man occupies a unique place in creation . . . in his own nature he unites the spiritual and material worlds.

— *Catechism of the Catholic Church* 41; 355

It must be emphasized again: throughout Western civilization, for more than seventeen centuries, this was the story that answered the most basic questions about where we came from, why we are here, how we are to view ourselves and others, how we are to live our lives. And, as such, this was the story that provided the *context* in which the individual stories of men and women were understood.

The implications of such a view of things are not hard to comprehend. In fact, they followed quite naturally from the basic elements of the story. And primary among them was this: knowledge of God's mind and will was the most important kind of knowledge. Learning how to build and fix a toaster — important and useful. Learning how to love God and neighbor and fulfill one's destiny for all eternity — more important, more useful.

Naturalism's Story

Now, within Western civilization, another story has come to take the place of the Christian theistic story, nearly its mirror opposite: the story of naturalism.

So how does this story go? It, too, begins at the beginning — as all stories that are intended to answer life's Big Questions ultimately must:

> In the beginning was the natural universe — matter and energy, and nothing more.

According to this story, we — and all other living things — have been created by the earth. We are the result of an entirely natural evolutionary process operating within an entirely natural universe. God does not exist, and we were not created in His image and likeness. There are neither spirits nor souls. The universe is, from first to last, a "natural" universe.

As with the older story, the implications of this newer story are also not hard to derive or comprehend. For instance, if God doesn't exist and did not create man in His image and likeness, then man must have created God in *his* image and likeness.

No wonder the God of Christians seems more like a man than anything else — an extraordinary man, but only the imaginary creation of man. Indeed, since nothing exists but nature, all religions that speak of the supernatural — of gods, spirits, or souls — must essentially be a species

> If God doesn't exist and did not create man in His image and likeness, then man must have created God in *his* image and likeness.

of delusion. No doubt religions are manifestations of man's deep desire and wish that the world and life had ultimate meaning and that when one dies, it is not the end. But, of course, in a purely natural universe — a universe in which man is essentially an accident — the world and life have no ultimate meaning; when one dies, it *is* the end.

According to the naturalist view of things, while religions may be useful for controlling human behavior, like a paddle is useful for controlling the behavior of a child or a whip the behavior of a slave; while religions may provide some level of comfort in a cold and ultimately impersonal material universe; while religions may be interesting and personally satisfying for some; objectively speaking, religion is nonsense. Why? Because according to the atheist-naturalist view of the cosmos, there simply is no creator-God out there to *be* known. This assertion is perfectly exemplified in the title of Richard Dawkins' recent book *The God Who Isn't There*.

Objectively speaking, then, a believer's claim to have knowledge of the Creator's mind, intentions, and desires borders on — if not outright crosses — the boundary of sheer madness. Rather, all true knowledge that can be had of this world and ourselves is knowledge obtained as we explore the world, and ourselves, rationally and scientifically.

Apologist Phillip Johnson sums up the naturalist's perspective:

> What we used to call knowledge of God (theology) is only human knowledge, since humans invented God to explain things before they had scientific

knowledge. A consequence of the "death of God," which is simply the realization that evolution is our real creator, is the realization that we can obtain knowledge only from science — including not only physics and biology but also the human sciences such as psychology, anthropology and sociology.[8]

THE RISE OF THE NEW STORY

Now, *how* the naturalist story came to replace the Christian theistic story is itself a long and involved story, one we can only touch on here.

It had to do with a naturalistic philosophy coming, over time, to dominate in the academic realms, especially in the sciences; then, over more time, coming to dominate in the realm of ideas in general. We might describe the process as a kind of sleight-of-hand: magicians in white lab coats equated science with naturalism, then declared naturalism to be true *on the merits of science*.

They began with an undeniably true assertion: that the scientific method, if used correctly, has been demonstrated to be a precise and trustworthy method of gaining accurate information about the natural world — as evidenced by remarkable successes and innumerable stunning advances in the fields of medicine, engineering, manufacturing, and technology. But where the "magic" occurred is when they moved from this true assertion to one undeniably false: that science and naturalism *are somehow essentially the same thing*. From this, they drew the preposterous conclusion that *because science has been demonstrated as true, naturalism has also been demonstrated as true.*

> We're thrilled not to have to sit in a medieval dentist's chair or drive around like Fred Flintstone, using our feet to accelerate and brake our vehicles.

Now, with the first assertion, we have absolutely no beef; in fact, we're thrilled not to have to sit in a medieval dentist's chair or drive around like Fred Flintstone, using our feet to accelerate and brake our vehicles. The scientific method has demonstrated its value. No debate here.

The problem is in the second and third assertions — that science and naturalism are in some way to be equated, that the two are somehow essentially the same thing, and therefore, that naturalism slips in on the lab coattails of science.

In fact, the two are quite distinct. Whereas science is a *method* for investigating the natural world, naturalism is a *philosophy* that says the natural world *is all there is*.

So the question a perceptive person might want to ask the magician is this: how exactly does your investigation of the natural world lead you to the conclusion that the natural world is all there is? Or, to put it another way: since science only deals with the examination of nature, if something other than or outside nature existed — for instance, God — would it not by definition be *outside the realm of what science investigates?* How, then, could science come to determine that God doesn't exist — when God is outside its realm? In fact, how could science say *anything at all* about the subject of God's existence?

But this is precisely what modern atheists assert in their arguments for the cause of naturalism — that, in some fashion, science has ruled out God or shown conclusively that the natural world is all that exists.

Thus, their entire framework of thought and argumentation rests on the single *sine qua non* premise that God doesn't exist. To them, this conclusion seems ineluctably logical. (After all, hasn't science proven it?) But if they are wrong about that, then the whole naturalist theory collapses as any kind of viable explanation for the existence of everything. And that's a key "if" in the equation.

What would we think of an auto mechanic who concluded from his intensive study of cars that nothing existed but cars? A kind man might say this mechanic has wandered a bit from his field of expertise. Others might say he's lost his mind. So let's just say that the scientist who concludes from his study of nature that nature is all that exists has wandered just a bit from his field of expertise. And yet, surveys (such as a 1998 poll conducted by *Nature* Magazine) show that a vast preponderance of American scientists identify themselves as atheists, most of them declaring their rejection of God's existence *on the basis of science.*[9]

The question of whether God exists, or whether nature is all there is, is a strictly *philosophical* question. Its answer cannot be determined by the use of the scientific method or scientific instruments. One wouldn't think to use a microscope to discover whether right and wrong exist, or a slide-rule to determine if courage is a virtue. Likewise, the fact that science has not stumbled over God in the forest or been able to cook up a batch of angels in a test tube means nothing at all with regard to the question of whether or not God or angels exist. If God and angels were material substances, it might . . . but they're *not*.

Yet naturalism is still considered to be somehow "proven" by science.

"UNENLIGHTENED" BELIEVERS

A concomitant opinion also prevails among an increasingly large number of moderns who consider themselves scientifically "enlightened" — that whoever *denies* naturalism and all its ramifications is just uneducated. Exemplifying this attitude — so prevalent in the scientific establishment — is this excerpt from a short piece written by Jesse Bering, director of the Institute of Cognition and Culture at Queen's University, Belfast:

> With each meticulous turn of the screw in science, with each tightening up of our understanding of the natural world, we pull more taut the straps over God's muzzle. From botany to bioengineering, from physics to psychology, what is science really but true revelation? We bravely favor truth, in all its wondrous, amoral, and meaningless complexity, over the singularly destructive Truth born of the trembling minds of our ancestors.[10]

Notice, again, the sleight-of-hand? His absurd argument here could be summarized thus: As *science* (a method of examination) comes to understand the natural world better (the object of scientific examination), somehow *naturalism* (the philosophical position which asserts that nothing exists but the natural world) is shown to be *true*. And thus people are expected to accept the claim that God is nothing but a concept, a fanciful notion, an idea "born of the trembling minds of our ancestors." Obviously, though, no such vindication of naturalism has been (or could be) rendered using that kind of illogic.

> People are expected to accept the claim that God is nothing but a concept, a fanciful notion, an idea "born of the trembling minds of our ancestors."

No doubt, Mr. Bering feels he has delivered a knockout punch against theism here. And no wonder — when in one corner of the ring, weighing in with heavy academic credentials, we find the scientist, bravely favoring "truth in all its amoral and meaningless complexity." In the other corner of the ring? Only the "trembling mind" of the hopelessly ignorant and befuddled believer in God.

THE PREVALENCE OF NATURALISM

And so the age-old Christian theistic story has been steadily losing ground in the battle for public opinion, to the point that naturalism has already taken its place as the "official" story of our modern secular age. This is the story our children are being taught in our schools and great universities. This is the story vast numbers of people in the West now simply assume to have been demonstrated as true.

Now, with this change in the "macro" story by which we understand and make sense of the "micro" stories of our individual lives has come an understandable change in the way our society views many things. One example would be the modern understanding of human sexuality, marriage, and the meaning of family.

Before, under the reign of the Christian theistic story, the personal God was at the heart of everything; questions about these issues could not be answered without reference to our creation in God's image and without regard for His intentions (i.e., commandments). Believing the Christian theistic story, the most natural questions in the world to ask included: What does it mean to say that God has created us in His image as male and female? What is the purpose of human sexuality? What is marriage for? What other ethical issues might guide us in our understanding?

But now, under the reign of naturalism, everything has changed. If, as the famous nineteenth-century atheist Friedrich Nietzsche proclaimed, "God is dead," and nothing exists but nature, then, of course, all this talk about "ultimate meaning" and "higher purposes" (in other words, all this "God talk") goes straight out the window. God has nothing whatsoever to do with these issues. Now marriage, family, and human sexuality need to be viewed through the lens of evolutionary biology, sociology, and psychology. The conclusion follows seamlessly: we once looked to God, but now we should abandon outmoded ways of thinking (i.e., looking to God) and look to science to assist us in forming our own personal perspectives on what is normal and good.

This is one example; this same pattern of change can be seen everywhere as, throughout the modern world, naturalism continues to replace Christian theism as the accepted view of "how things really are."

CONFLICTING WORLDVIEWS

We've been speaking of two stories. But, in philosophical terms, we're talking about two *worldviews* — two systems of thought, two ways of looking at our world and ourselves within it. And notice the total opposition in which these worldviews, these systems of thought, stand in relation to each other.

If the naturalist worldview is true, then the Christian theistic worldview is not true. Then, those of us who believe in God are deluded, living in a fantasy world. Then, our view of the world is fundamentally *irrational* in the sense that it is not in accord with reason and separated from reality. Then, what we rear our children to believe — that they are created and loved by God and ought to live in accordance with God's laws — is actually harmful to them. It cuts them off from the truth of who they really are and what life is really about. It teaches them to chase illusions. We might as well teach them to offer sacrifice to the Smurfs, pray to the Tooth Fairy, and live according to the rules of morality laid down by Santa Claus. All of which, of course, would be ludicrously meaningless and utterly futile.

> We might as well teach them to offer sacrifice to the Smurfs, pray to the Tooth Fairy, and live according to the rules of morality laid down by Santa Claus.

This is essentially how ideologically committed atheists view those who believe spiritual realties such as God, Jesus Christ, the sacraments, the inspiration of Scripture, and the like. In their eyes, it is just as much superstitious nonsense for a Christian to kneel down and pray to God as it would be for someone to kneel down and pray to Papa Smurf.

But, of course, the converse would also follow. If the Christian theistic worldview is *true*, then the naturalist worldview is not true; it would be as patently ludicrous to *deny* the existence of God as it would be to deny the tangible reality of this book that you hold in your hands right now. If God does exist, then it is the atheist-naturalist who is deluded. If God exists, then it is *the atheist's* view of the world that is contrary to reason and a fundamental denial of reality. If God exists, then the religion of science and naturalism, in which he rears his children and whose tenets he teaches them to believe and live by, is false and futile because it completely misses the truth. The atheist parent inculcates in his children — and the atheist teacher in his students — the notion that they are simply the product of an impersonal, blind, wholly random natural evolutionary process. He teaches them that there is no God and no moral law and that they will need to decide for themselves what they feel is right and wrong. Of course, if God does exist, then this training in the blind faith of atheism is supremely harmful to those children; it cuts them off from the truth of who they really are and what life is really about. In short, if God does exist, then atheism is nothing better than a Godless delusion — a fundamental disconnection from reality.

Obviously, we believe that this is precisely what atheism is, and we will endeavor to demonstrate this fact as we proceed. As we will see, in spite of all the incessant bobbing and weaving in which atheist arguments against God engage, they will be knocked for a loop as the case for belief in God lands the uppercuts, right hooks, and other counter-punches that are the rational *reasons* for theism.

CHAPTER TWO

A SOLUTION TO THE DELUSION

Ever since the creation of the world his invisible nature, namely, his eternal power and deity, *has been clearly perceived in the things that have been made.*

— Rom 1:20 (emphasis added)

As an atheistic, naturalist worldview makes steady progress in driving the Christian theistic worldview from the philosophical stage of Western civilization, Christians must learn how to vigorously defend the truth of God's existence. And more to the point: Christians must learn how to forcefully *expose* the lie of atheistic naturalism.

The curtain may appear to be drawing on Christian society in the West — but, as those who believe in God know, the story isn't over.

A GOOD OFFENSE

Too often, Catholics and other Christians accept the role assigned them by modern secular consensus: that we — not the atheists — are the ones in the position of having to defend what is rationally indefensible. We're the ones who sometimes feel embarrassed by our supposedly "unscientific" worldview. It's our assigned role, we tacitly agree, to receive the hardball questions being hurled at us by the modern, scientific, "enlightened" world — "I've never seen God. Show me the evidence of his existence! You believe that Christ performed miracles and rose from

the dead? Show me the scientific proof that miracles occur
or that the dead can rise!" — and answer them. Often
Christians who believe in God, but aren't exactly sure what
the arguments might be for the reasonableness of their faith,
accept an inferior position in the debate, even admitting
at times that their beliefs are *not* something that could be
rationally demonstrated. They retreat into pure fideism
(from the Latin word for "faith"), hang their heads, and
feebly confess, "I don't know, you just have to believe!"

Well, it's about time the tables were turned. It's about
time believers came to realize that it is the Christian,
not the naturalist, worldview that makes sense of our
experience as human beings. In contract, it is naturalism
that is unreasonable, that cannot make sense of even the
most basic aspects of human experience, that unravels
(pardon the threadbare metaphor) "like a cheap suit" when
examined and questioned.

Therefore, it is naturalism that needs to be on the
defensive.

It is often said, "The best defense is a good offense."
We intend in the chapters to follow to apply this dictum
aggressively to the question at hand. We intend to show
that, however accepted the naturalist worldview may have
become throughout our modern society and civilization,
it simply isn't true. Atheistic naturalism is a lie, a lie that
can be exposed.

PRESUPPOSITIONAL APOLOGETICS

This book is an exercise in what is called the
presuppositional approach to Christian apologetics. It is an

eminently practical approach, one that can be used freely in the real-life situations in which you will inevitably find yourself when opportunities to share the truth with God-deniers arise.

So what is the presuppositional approach?

When Christian apologists argue "presuppositionally," we seek to compare and contrast the theistic and naturalist worldviews, in order to show our atheist friend that while our worldview makes sense of human experience, his does not.

We want to demonstrate that while the Christian worldview *can account for and make sense of* the most basic and important aspects of his experience as a human being, the atheist worldview simply cannot. Naturalists who say that nothing exists but matter cannot make sense of realities such as the existence of right and wrong, the possibility of knowledge, or the belief in human dignity, freedom, and personality. In this way, we hope to lead our unbelieving friend to see that he must, in fact, *presuppose* God's existence in order to make heads or tails of his experience as a human being.

Our argument is that God's existence *alone* provides the very preconditions of intelligible human experience. We contend that *the denial of God's existence* leads to the complete disintegration of not only morality, meaning, and human value and dignity, but the possibility of knowledge itself. The atheist worldview leads to foolishness. It leads to conclusions the atheist is not going to be willing or able to live with.

In short, we seek to demonstrate God's existence by showing conclusively the *impossibility of the contrary*. The atheist, we shall see, must presuppose God's existence even to argue against it.

An important logical tool in your apologetics toolbox is called the *reductio ad absurdum* (reducing to absurdity). This tool is at the heart of the presuppositional apologetic method. The *reductio ad absurdum* method logically demonstrates that seemingly plausible or superficially true claims can be proven to be false simply by reducing them to their absurd necessary conclusions. No matter how attractive the ideas may be, in the end they are still untenable. The *reductio ad absurdum* works with razor-sharp effectiveness when applied properly to the atheist-naturalist worldview, as we intend to demonstrate in the pages that follow: atheism, literally, reduces to absurdity.

In practice, the presuppositional method entails stepping into the atheist's worldview and performing an internal critique. And lovingly, gently — but ruthlessly — reducing it to its unavoidably absurd conclusions.

The resulting criticisms are, as you will see, intolerable and therefore untenable for the atheist. The challenge is to stay the course long enough for the atheist to realize this.

CREATION REVEALS THE CREATOR

Although it is tempting at this point to leap directly into our critique of the naturalist worldview, first, we need to flesh out the nature of our apologetic approach a bit further by looking at Scripture. As it turns out, we can learn much about how to carry out the apologetic task as Christians by looking at what God's Word teaches us about the world God created, as well as about the atheist we seek to evangelize.

First, Scripture teaches us that God exists. "In the beginning God . . ."

Second, Scripture teaches us that God created the cosmos and everything in it.

> In the beginning, God created the heavens and the earth. . . . "Let us make man in our image, after our likeness . . ."
>
> — Gen. 1:1, 26

Notice here that, according to Scripture, the atheist is in the image and likeness of God as much as St. Thomas Aquinas or St. Francis of Assisi. This is going to become crucially important along the way: the atheist, whatever he may say about the world, is what he is: a human being created specifically to mirror the God who created him. He is an image, a likeness, of God.

Third, Scripture teaches us that all creation gives evidence for God's existence. For instance, as Psalm 19:1-3 tells us:

> The heavens are telling the glory of God; and the firmament proclaims his handiwork. Day to day pours forth speech, and night to night declares knowledge. There is no speech, nor are there words; their voice is not heard; yet their voice goes out through all the earth, and their words to the ends of the world.

We see this also in Romans 1:20:

> Ever since the creation of the world his invisible
> nature, namely, his eternal power and deity, *has been
> clearly perceived* in the things that have been made.[11]

Now, Scripture has much more to teach us that will provide important preparation for the apologetic task before us, but we can start with these three basic Scriptural premises: (1) God exists. (2) God created the cosmos and everything in it. (3) The cosmos and everything in it points to the existence of God.

Whether or not one accepts these premises as *true*, they are certainly *internally coherent:* they make basic intuitive sense. Even as it makes basic intuitive sense to think that a building will evidence the existence of its builder, so it makes basic intuitive sense to think that if God created, as Nehemiah said, "the heavens, the heaven of heavens, with all their host, the earth and all that is on it, the seas and all that is in them" (9:6) — then, all creation would evidence God's existence.

That which is created speaks of its creator.

Take, for example, the book *God Is Not Great*, written by the famous British atheist Christopher Hitchens. Now, we would argue that Hitchens' book, written specifically to make the case against the existence of God, in fact very eloquently makes the *opposite* case (see Chapter Six). But for now, we should be able to agree that, at the very least, Hitchens' book makes the case for the existence of Hitchens. A book speaks of its author, and everyone accepts on face value that Christopher Hitchens is the author of *God Is Not Great*. Hitchens' name is emblazoned on the front cover; his picture adorns its dust cover. At book signings for *God Is Not Great*, Hitchens is the one doing the signing. Everyone who knows of this book knows that it was authored — *created*, one might say — by Christopher Hitchens.

Furthermore, the evidence that Hitchens wrote the book is not simply on the cover but written, literally, on every page. One would imagine that those who know Christopher Hitchens personally have little problem finding countless clear evidences not only of the author's existence but also of his personality, style of writing, use of language, sense of humor, philosophy of life, methods of argumentation, and much more on every page.

The book *God Is Not Great* "cries out" the existence of its author in every way, as well as revealing something of his nature, character, and personality.

But imagine for a moment that someone denied that Hitchens wrote the book. Imagine this person claimed that the book called *God Is Not Great*, which you see sitting on that table over there, is the result of an explosion in a print factory. Or imagine he says that the book is simply the accidental result of an excruciatingly long, random process of various molecules and compounds combining, dissolving, and recombining endlessly. This process, it is argued, involved relentless blind forces of nature that acted upon random collections of elements. And that the book you now see — every word, sentence, paragraph, and chapter — is simply the form these molecules happen to have taken at this particular moment in time.

The book *God Is Not Great* "cries out" the existence of its author in every way, as well as revealing something of his nature, character, and personality.

Can you imagine anyone dumb enough to accept that claim? Can you imagine anyone wasting any time pondering the possibility that Christopher Hitchens did not write the book, which just happens to bear his name on its cover and in its copyright statement, and happens to have his picture on the dust cover? No, of course not.

No one would give credence to such a claim because it is common knowledge that books do not come into existence as a result of random, blind forces of nature. Authors write books, and we can know much about the author from the book he wrote.

CREATION IS NO ACCIDENT

We believe that God created the world according to his wisdom. It is not the product of any necessity whatever, nor of blind fate or chance. We believe that it proceeds from God's free will; he wanted to make his creatures share in his being, wisdom and goodness.

— *Catechism of the Catholic Church* 295

The Catholic critique of atheism, therefore, is twofold:

1) God created the cosmos and, therefore, the cosmos and everything in it evidences God's existence and nature;

2) If God does not exist, the cosmos is irretrievably unintelligible.

The central thesis of the "Godless delusion" is not simply that God's existence alone can adequately account for the existence and complexity of the cosmos; it is based on the fact that God's existence is a *sine qua non* for explaining anything *at all*.

Humanity itself remains forever inexplicable when seen through the lens of atheistic naturalism. It is the Christian theistic lens that brings everything into sharp focus, enabling us to make sense of both ourselves and our place within the cosmos.

CONVINCING FACTS

It makes sense to think that every fact of creation, if understood and interpreted correctly, demonstrates the existence of the God who created all things.

But Christians may be tempted to grant to the naturalist that God's existence is not all that evident from what God has made. We sometimes fall into thinking that only certain kinds of facts are convincing evidences of God's existence — facts like the Resurrection of Christ or the stigmata of Padre Pio, things we can set forth as "miraculous" and contrary to nature (as if nature itself were not miraculous). But notice that St. Paul does not grant to the atheist that the evidence of God's existence is either ambiguous or equivocal. Rather, he insists that God's existence is "*clearly perceived* in the things that have been made" (Rom. 1:20).

And if God created everything, then it makes sense to think that every "thing" — every real being — would reveal the existence of the God who made it. It makes sense to think that, at least in principle, any and every fact in the world could be used as an argument for God's existence. Although Psalm 19 speaks of the "heavens" as declaring the glory of God, one could just as well speak of the green grass, or Mozart's music, or Grandma's crazy laugh, or the look of wonder in the eyes of a toddler seeing the ocean for the first time, as "crying out" the existence of God. Is any one of these more or less miraculous than the other? Does any one of these speak more or less of the God who made them?

Psalm 19:1-3 tells us that creation speaks of God's existence continuously ("Day to day pours forth speech, and night to night declares knowledge"), and that the message comes to every person on the face of the earth ("There is no speech, nor are there words; their voice is not heard; yet their voice goes out through all the earth, and their words to the ends of the world"). To paraphrase the psalm, the voice of the cosmos calls out with words that go out to the ends of the world, communicating to every human being the truth about the God who created it. Again, even as a book tells you much about its author, so it is with the stars and planets, oceans and forests, animals and the plants we see all around us — and especially, human beings, who are the image and likeness of God himself. Each of them individually and all of them corporately speak to us of God's existence. And, through their beauty and order, they tell us a great deal about what kind of person He is.

We get the message. But in Romans 1:18-20, Scripture goes on to teach us as a fourth truth: This message of creation, this argument for God's existence — it *gets through* to human beings. Even the atheist knows in his heart of hearts the God who created him and everything else.

> For the wrath of God is revealed from heaven against all ungodliness and unrighteousness of men, who *suppress* the truth in unrighteousness, because that which may be known about God is *evident within them*; for God made it *evident to them*. For since the creation of the world His invisible attributes, His eternal power and divine nature, have been *clearly seen*, being *understood* through what has been made, so that they are *without excuse*.[12]
>
> — Rom 1:18-20 (NIV)

Whether or not someone is willing to admit it, he "gets it" when he encounters nature's voice proclaiming the existence of the God who created it. It's not that God's existence is merely "suggested" through what has been made, or faintly "hinted at." St. Paul says it is *clearly seen*. In fact, he says God's existence and nature are so clearly recognizable that men and women who refuse to acknowledge Him are *without excuse*. (Remember, it's just like someone looking at a book and insisting that it had no author but was merely the random chance of forces of nature. Everyone would laugh at that notion, and no one would take him seriously. That's how clear it is that there is a God.)

This leads us to a fifth point Scripture makes: those who would deny God's existence must actually *suppress* the abundance of evidence all around them in order to avoid believing in God — in order to avoid God himself. That's right. Atheists must deny reality, day in and day out, in order to maintain some semblance of continuity for themselves and their inherently self-contradictory worldview.

Think back to a time in your life (we've all been there) when you willfully suppressed the truth with a lie. Doing this made you uncomfortable, perhaps even miserable — and the bigger the lie you told, the worse it made you feel, right?

Atheists are in a similar predicament. All of creation cries out the existence and glory of God, so much so that in order to escape God, the unbeliever must engage in a massive and continual suppression of the evidences seen in His creation.

> In order to escape God, the unbeliever must engage in a massive and continual suppression of the evidences seen in His creation.

And this denial calls for more than simply suppressing external evidence, the voice of creation. St. Paul says, "That which may be known about God is *evident within them.*" Read those words again. Ponder them. "That which may be known about God is *evident within them*" (or, *within you*). Not only does the atheist live in a world in which he cannot look up or down, right or left without being confronted by the evidences for God's existence and essential character; he is *himself the very image and likeness of God,* created to reflect the being of God in a unique way. Even if he were blind and had never seen the heavens declaring the glory of God, even if he were deaf and had never heard a human voice, he could not escape the reality of God. For he himself is the most powerful argument of all in favor of God's existence.[13]

Whatever an atheist may *say* about the world, he is still a manifestation of the image and likeness of God. He bears in his own being the most powerful proofs of God's existence and information about His nature. If he closes his eyes to escape into the solitude of his own mind and heart, he is immediately confronted with the clearest of all evidences — his own being.

ATHEISM'S FOLLY

Lastly, Scripture says that atheism is the ultimate foolishness. Psalm 14:1 tells us, "The fool says in his heart, 'There is no God.'"

While we don't at all relish the idea of calling anyone a "fool," objectively speaking, what other word but "foolishness" can be used to describe the condition of one who has been created by God, whose very being is in every aspect a walking advertisement for God's existence, who lives in a universe in which every single fact speaks to him continuously of the God who made all things, who in his heart of hearts knows the true God, but who then suppresses all these evidences, erases the truth from his mind, and claims that God doesn't exist at all?

The atheist, Scripture teaches us, is like a man sauntering down the Champs-Elysées in Paris wearing on his head an ancient, famous, one-of-a-kind crown worn by French kings, carrying with him three Van Gogh originals — yet when police stop him for questioning, he vigorously insists that he did not steal the treasures from the museum across the street. He's like a child sitting on the swing set in the backyard of his home on a Saturday afternoon, sipping from a cool glass of lemonade, listening to the sound of the vacuum cleaner coming through the kitchen window, enjoying the smell of hot dogs cooking on the patio grill, and discussing with his little sister whether or not their parents, who love them, exist.

Atheism is not simply a denial of God's existence. As a practical matter, it forces atheists to *live* in denial. Atheists are walking, talking contradictions, much like the string of words on a page that reads: "This sentence is not true." The incoherence lurking at the heart of atheism's denial of God produces endless inconsistencies. The atheist who proclaims, "God does not exist!" is much like a man who declares, "I am not speaking."

This is the bleak and pitiful situation of the atheist — hopelessly tangled in his own denial of reality.

Well, perhaps not exactly *hopelessly*. As we shall see, there are ways to help the atheist extricate himself from his God-denying dilemma.

UNDERSTANDING ATHEISTS

Grasping the nature of the atheist dilemma is of paramount importance for Catholics and other Christians who seek to help atheists out of the darkness of disbelief and into the light of truth.

For a moment, imagine a man who conducted public lectures on the subject that there is no gravity and wrote best-selling books denying its existence. What conclusions would you be able to draw about this man? What would you know about him even before speaking to him?

Well, first of all, you would know that he was deluding himself. Gravity exists, whether he likes it or not, and the evidence of its existence is all around him. Every time he takes a step and his foot hits the ground, he proves that gravity exists. Every time he drops a quarter and it doesn't stay suspended in midair, his position is refuted. And the very fact that he doesn't chain himself to the floor when delivering his lectures, or glue his notes to the podium while speaking, implicitly demonstrates that *he knows* gravity exists. He can deny the existence of gravity all he wants, but he is forced — whether he will acknowledge it or not — to *live* according to the law of gravity.

But there is something else you would know about your gravity-denying friend: You would know that his position was foolishness because it doesn't fit the real world. If he were to really try to *live* according to what he *says* he believes about the world, the folly of his position would become apparent immediately. It wouldn't take many experiments stepping out of third-story windows or out of airplanes in mid-flight for him to quickly discover the error of his thinking.

Finally, notice the tension the poor fellow must endure. On the one hand, he claims that gravity doesn't exist, writes books and gives lectures that no doubt offer elaborate proofs for the non-existence of gravity. And yet on the other hand he must live every day in the real world where every step he takes contradicts his position and proves him wrong.

This is the atheist's predicament. He lives in tension. He claims there is no God, but he has no choice but to live in the world God created, the real world, a world that calls out to him from every direction the truth of God's existence. If he tried to live out his atheism consistently, the foolishness of his position would become apparent immediately. But he does not, because he cannot — any more than the gravity-denier can live out his position consistently.

When you sit down to share a cup of coffee or a glass of wine with someone who denies the existence of God, from the teaching of Scripture you can know two things about him right from the start: First, you can know that your friend is deluding himself. He knows that God exists, and he even knows something of who God is. How could he not, knowing himself and knowing others who are the image and likeness of God? He may have worked hard for a long time to suppress that knowledge, but he knows. Second, you can know that your friend's worldview is incapable of allowing him to make sense of his experience in the real world.

You can know these things about the atheist right up front, in the same way you would know them about a man who claimed not to believe in gravity.

In the end, the atheist can "deny" God's existence, but he cannot stop being the image and likeness of God. Therefore, he cannot help evidencing God's existence, even in the act of disavowing it. As we shall see, even his ability to reason about the existence of God proves him wrong. Indeed, his very ability to say, "There is no God" refutes his error.

And so, the atheist lives in the conflict of his self-imposed exile from reality. He cannot avoid the God he claims is not there. And, as converts from atheism will tell you, deep down in his heart of hearts, this realization drives him crazy. This explains why so many atheists are so tub-thumping angry with people who openly profess their belief in God. Atheists, as the old saying goes, "want to have their cake and eat it, too" — only they don't want theists to have any cake at all.

CHAPTER THREE

THE DEATH OF RIGHT AND WRONG

Moral properties constitute so odd a cluster of properties and relations that they are most unlikely to have arisen in the ordinary course of events without an all-powerful god to create them.

— J. L. Mackie

Everyone has heard the blithely optimistic saying, "It's always darkest just before the dawn." That's how most of us prefer to approach life's problems — hopeful that, no matter how bad things might be, they will soon get better. But when it comes to predicting the extent of atheism's increasingly deleterious impact on the West in the coming decades, such optimism seems out of place. Those familiar with the darkly humorous demotivational posters produced by the company Despair, Inc.,[14] have seen one whose sentiment may be more accurate to the current situation: "It's always darkest just before it goes pitch black."

As bad as things are now with the rising tide of atheist-naturalist ideology inundating the mental coastlines of the Western mind, things could get considerably worse unless Christians do something about it. The more proficient Christians become at dismantling the clever yet vacuous arguments raised by God-deniers, and demonstrating the emptiness — indeed, foolishness — of the atheist-naturalist worldview, the less their ideas will hold sway in modern society.

And, of course, the converse is equally true: To the extent that Christians sit back in complacency or trepidation and do nothing to respond to atheist challenges, atheism will conquer the West as surely as fire will burn down a forest.

Because the naturalist worldview has effectively supplanted Christian theism as the approved, "officially sanctioned" worldview of the secular West, those Big Questions that human beings in every generation wonder about — *What is reality? What does it mean to be human? Who am I? How did I get here, and where am I going after this life?* — are being answered incorrectly and with devastating effect. Without the correct answers to such questions, and the interpretive context and meaning to what can seem like an endless series of events from birth to death, men and women won't be able to make sense of their individual lives. And make no mistake: while it may not be explicitly stated in every high school and college science class or on every science museum display, the naturalist worldview is assumed to be true and presented as such.

NATURALISM'S FUNDAMENTAL FLAW

In this chapter, we begin in earnest our internal critique of the naturalist worldview. Our basic approach will be to compare and contrast the Christian theistic and naturalist worldviews — to hold both macro stories up to the light and ask the following question: Which worldview is able to make sense of our experience as human beings? Atheists, of course, will confidently claim that theirs does. No matter. We intend to show that the naturalist worldview does not and, indeed, cannot make good on that claim.

By contrast, our claim is that the Christian theistic worldview *does* provide a basis for essential aspects of human experience. In fact, the moment one assumes the existence of God, and God's creation of men and women in His image and likeness, everything else falls into place. Banish God from the universe and morality, knowledge, human dignity, freedom, and meaning are banished with Him.

> Banish God from the universe and morality, knowledge, human dignity, freedom, and meaning are banished with Him.

Ironically, in order for the atheist's life not to descend into utter chaos, he actually must live as though the Christian theistic worldview were true, even as he denies God's existence. He *has* been created in God's image, and so knows in his heart of hearts that knowledge is possible, that right and wrong are real, and that life has meaning.

Conceptually, atheists take for granted that God doesn't exist. In the words of the famous TV news anchorman Walter Cronkite, "That's the way it is": *no God, just the natural world I see around me.* But practically speaking, atheists really don't *live* according to that notion. They cannot.

To make that case, let's start by examining what naturalists believe.

From the *Encyclopedia of Philosophy*:

> Naturalism is . . . defined as repudiating the view that there exists or could exist any entities or events which lie, in principle, beyond the scope of scientific

explanation. The entire knowable universe is composed of natural objects — that is, objects which come into and pass out of existence in consequence of the operation of "natural causes." A rock, a cloud, a frog, a human being, are all instances of natural objects, however they may otherwise differ and however important these differences may be. . . . Naturalism [holds] that whatever exists or happens is natural in the sense of being susceptible to explanation through methods which are continuous from domain to domain of objects and events. . . . Hence, knowledge of the world at any given time is what science tells us at that time about the world.[15]

Another term commonly used to describe the naturalist worldview is "materialism," which the *Merriam-Webster Dictionary* defines as:

A theory that physical matter is the only or fundamental reality and that all being and processes and phenomena can be explained as manifestations or results of matter.

Most people use the word "materialism" these days to speak of the love of material possessions. (Remember Madonna's hit song from the early '80s, "Material Girl"?) To avoid confusion, then, we use the world "naturalism" to describe the atheistic worldview that says nothing exists but natural objects, material, particles.

The *Encyclopedia of Philosophy* definition of materialism makes it clear that "materialism" and "naturalism" are really two words to describe the same worldview.

Materialism asserts that the real world consists of material things, and nothing else. Therefore, there are no incorporeal souls or spirits, no spiritual principalities or powers, no angels or devils, no gods . . . The second major tenet of materialism is, accordingly: everything that can be explained can be explained on the basis of laws involving only antecedent physical conditions [physical laws, laws operating within the natural realm].[16]

These definitions provide us with the basic framework of assumptions that underlie the atheist-naturalist worldview: Nothing exists but the natural world, the realm of material objects. All natural objects or entities — including you and me — come into existence and pass out of existence by purely natural causes and processes. There is no God who creates and directs things, and therefore there are no such entities as spirits or souls. Nothing exists or (get this!) *can* exist that might "lie, in principle, beyond the scope of scientific explanation." Everything can be explained purely on the basis of physical laws operating within the natural realm, which is all that exists. Therefore, "knowledge of the world at any given time is what science tells us at that time about the world."

THE ASCENDANCY OF NATURALISM

If you believe in God, you no doubt reflexively recoil from that set of claims, and rightly so. But this is the view of things to which an increasing number of educated people today cling tenaciously. And the *Encyclopedia of Philosophy* bears this out when it reports, "The triumphant progress in the twentieth century of a materialist biology and biochemistry has almost completely eliminated . . . supernatural views of life."[17]

While we do not, of course, agree that this state of affairs amounts to anything close to "progress," we admit that it does represent a resounding triumph for atheism. The Godless delusion is alive and well and making converts left and right.

This is a dismal situation, to be sure, but not an incurable one.

To flesh out and illustrate what we're saying here, we will begin by examining some important aspects of human experience and see what happens to them if we assume the truth of the naturalist worldview. We begin with the issue of morality.

RULES OF FAIR PLAY

C. S. Lewis begins his classic work *Mere Christianity* by arguing that everyone seems to believe in the existence of what he refers to as a "law of morality." It appears, he says, that everyone believes in Right and Wrong — not merely as words we use to describe the things of which we approve or disapprove, or what we like or dislike, but as a real standard that somehow exists in the real world. We demonstrate this belief continually in the way we speak.

The passage is a bit long, but it's worth reading carefully.

> Everyone has heard people quarrelling. . . . They say things like this: . . . 'That's my seat, I was there first'
> . . . 'Leave him alone, he isn't doing you any harm'
> . . . 'Give me a bit of your orange, I gave you a bit of

mine' . . . 'Come on, you promised.' . . . Now what interests me about all these remarks is that the man who makes them is not merely saying that the other man's behavior does not happen to please him. He is appealing to some kind of standard of behavior which he expects the other man to know about. And the other man very seldom replies: 'To hell with your standard.' Nearly always he tries to make out that what he has been doing does not really go against the standard, or that if it does there is some special excuse. . . . It looks, in fact, very much as if both parties had in mind some kind of Law or Rule of fair play or decent behavior or morality or whatever you like to call it, about which they really agreed. And they have. If they had not, they might, of course, fight like animals, but they could not quarrel in the human sense of the word. Quarrelling means trying to show that the other man is in the wrong. And there would be no sense in trying to do that unless you and he had some sort of agreement as to what Right and Wrong are; just as there would be no sense in saying that a footballer had committed a foul unless there was some agreement about the rules of football.[18]

Here is an aspect of our experience as human beings: apparently, we all believe in the existence of a law of morality.

C. S. Lewis says this applies to "educated people as well as uneducated, and children as well as grown-ups," and we would hasten to add that it applies as well to Christian as well as atheist, Buddhist as well as Muslim, Hindu as well as Jew. Each of us continually and inescapably demonstrates that we believe in a "higher" law of morality — something higher than our own opinions and preferences.

CONVENTIONS OR STANDARDS?

At this point, atheists will typically respond that what we call "right" and "wrong" are merely cultural norms or societal conventions that have evolved over time. They assert that the differences in morals from culture to culture and time to time proves the point. But all one has to do is cross an atheist to discover that he doesn't really believe what he says he believes. Again, quoting Lewis:

> Whenever you find a man who says he does not believe in a real Right and Wrong, you will find the same man going back on this a moment later. He may break his promise to you, but if you try breaking one to him, he will be complaining 'It's not fair' before you can say Jack Robinson. . . . Have they not let the cat out of the bag and shown that, whatever they say, they really know the Law of Nature just like anyone else?[19]

Ken tells the following story about an experience he had in college that vividly brought this truth home:

> In college my wife and I had an atheist professor of psychology. I remember him traipsing into the lecture hall one evening and beginning his lecture with these words: "Right and wrong do not exist. They are merely cultural conventions, words societies use to describe what they approve and disapprove of. And the proof is that morals differ from culture to culture. For instance, there are Eskimo tribes in which the elderly, when they are determined to be no longer useful to society, are

set on a block of ice and sent out into the ocean to starve to death. And for these people, this is good and right. It is their way, and who are we to speak against them?"

Now, I have no idea whether what he said about the Eskimo tribes was true or not, but this is what he said, and I'm fairly certain he would have said the same thing about primitive societies in Africa where cannibalism was practiced or in India, where the time-honored custom of *Sati* was widely observed, in which many widows were (willingly or unwillingly) burned alive on the funeral pyres of their deceased husbands. After all, as he had just explained: "right" and "wrong" don't really exist as some kind of higher moral law which all people everywhere and always are obliged to obey. Morals are simply societal conventions that differ from culture to culture. Morals are simply "their way" of looking at things. And who are we to stand in judgment? Right?

At any rate, I recall looking around the lecture hall and wondering at the fact that no one really seemed all that surprised by what they had just been told. I saw no raised eyebrows. Most were studiously taking notes, assuming, I supposed at the time, that what the professor had just said should be simply taken as true.

I thought to myself: *How extraordinary. If God exists, then obviously right and wrong could exist as moral law in the universe he created. By announcing that right and wrong do not exist, this man has simply walked into the room and announced that God **does not exist**.*

I raised my hand and when the professor called on me, I asked the following question: "Professor, if what you say is true, then does this mean we cannot say that what Hitler did was 'wrong'? Wouldn't it follow from what you've said about right and wrong not existing and morals being only societal conventions that the best we can do is say we don't agree with Hitler's view of things, that we don't like what he did?"

The professor began to step — almost stumble — backward toward the corner of the room. His face turned red. He looked for a moment as though he were deep in thought and finally replied: "Well, I suppose there are some things we agree on *enough* that they kind of really become . . . wrong."

Even this man — a man willing to announce as fact to a lecture hall filled with college students that right and wrong do not exist — could not escape *believing in* right and wrong. When confronted with the unpleasant logical conclusions of his stated worldview — conclusions he must necessarily draw if he is to be rigorously logical and consistent (something atheists typically pride themselves in) — he collapsed. He simply could not maintain the fiction that he believed right and wrong to be nothing more than cultural convention.

He was exposed in one of his Godless delusions.

If right and wrong *really are* merely cultural conventions and *really are* relative from society to society, then how could we ever say that one society was morally superior to another?

How *can* we argue, for instance, that modern liberal society is any better or more moral than Nazi society, or that the morals of a group like Habitat for Humanity are any better than those of Al-Qaeda? The moment we say that the morality taught in the Jewish synagogue down the street is superior to the morality taught to members of

If right and wrong really are merely cultural conventions, how can we argue that the morality of Habitat for Humanity is better than that of Al-Qaeda?

Columbian drug cartels, we are appealing to a standard of morality that exists independent of those societies — above them, if you will — and by which we believe we can measure them both. We are assuming the existence of an absolute moral measuring stick — a law of morality. But if there *are* no real standards, then isn't it nonsense for us to argue, say, that the murderers who perpetrated the September 11, 2001, terror attacks did anything "wrong"? Perhaps they simply live by a different set of conventions. And as the professor said, who are we to judge?

The truth is, we *all* believe in a law of morality. And even those who *say* that moral laws don't exist actually show by the way they think, speak, and live that they really do believe in them.

Even the atheist ethics professor believes in a law of morality. Sure, he may mock Christianity in his classroom, with its ignorant belief in "moral absolutes," but he instantly becomes a strict proponent of moral absolutes the moment someone cuts in line in front of him at the checkout counter. "This isn't *right!*" he complains to himself, if not to the "immoral" culprit who committed the "unjust" act. And it will do no good to say to him at that moment, "Hey, morals differ from culture to culture, and who's to judge?" He knows that right and wrong are real.

He just can't help his natural response to even a minor violation of the moral law that, in his heart of hearts, he knows exists. God has inscribed an innate sense of justice on his very soul. The atheist can't erase it simply by telling himself over and over again that right and wrong are merely conventions. Whatever he says he believes as an atheist, deep down, he cannot help but know the truth — even if he refuses to admit it to himself or anyone else.

NATURAL LAW — ENGRAVED BY GOD IN THE HEART

The natural law expresses the original moral sense that enables man to discern by reason the good and the evil, the truth and the lie. The natural law is written and engraved in the soul of each and every man. . . .

The natural law, present in the heart of each man and established by reason, is universal in its precepts and its authority extends to all men.

The natural law, the Creator's very good work, provides the solid foundation on which man can build the structure of moral rules to guide his choices.

The Ten Commandments . . . are fundamentally immutable, and they oblige always and everywhere. No one can dispense from them. The Ten Commandments are engraved by God in the human heart.

— *Catechism of the Catholic Church* 1954; 1956; 1959; 2072

INTUITIVE MORALITY

It seems undeniable that we all believe in right and wrong — not merely as words we use to express our own personal preferences or tastes, or our society's evolved preferences or tastes, but as something that has real existence, something that applies to all people everywhere and at all times, something that *everyone ought to know.*

All of this fits beautifully with the Christian worldview. It makes perfect sense of our experience. It explains the existence of a moral law and why we all intuitively know it.

Christians hold that an infinite, personal God exists, a God who has a particular nature and moral character, if you will. And so, moral laws reflect the nature of *who God is.* God's character provides the source for morality as well as the standard for moral law in the universe He created. And since every human being is made in God's image, like God, we are moral beings. It's no wonder we know intuitively that right and wrong exist. It's no wonder we sense to the very core of our beings that right and wrong are somehow "real things," not simply words we use to express our personal preferences; God has written these fundamental moral laws on our very souls.

THE STANDARD OF GOODNESS

According to St. Thomas Aquinas, to say that God "is good" is really an expression of the fact that God is goodness itself.[20] "God [is] the absolute good, from whom all things are called good by participation."[21] This means that God is the perfection of goodness, and it is in comparison with that perfect standard that we can measure all relative goodness.

Here's another way to look at this. Picture in your mind a slightly crooked line — not straight, but *nearly* straight. The only way you could discern just how straight the line is would be to know what a truly straight line looks like. You have an *ideal* straight line against which all other lines can be compared. If you don't presuppose the ideal of a perfectly straight line, it's impossible for you to talk about other lines that are "more" or "less" straight.

This analogy can be duplicated in many different ways, such as the concept of a perfect circle as the standard against which someone can say, "That circle over there is slightly off." Again, the only way he can measure this is to have the ideal of a perfect circle with which to compare and contrast it.

This is the same principle we employ when talking about things being more or less "good." Without presupposing an absolute standard of "good" (which is God), there would be no way to discuss how near or far something is in relation to that standard.

When Christians speak about God being all good, then, it is not as though "right" and "wrong" are arbitrary concepts based on the arbitrary divine will — as if God could have just as easily commanded us to believe that, for example, the rape and murder of innocent children is good, or to admire cowardice, lying, and theft as ideals to be emulated. No. Right and wrong reflect the nature, the moral character, of God.

As you read these words, whether you are an atheist or a believer, isn't it true that you instinctively know in your heart, prior to anything we have said in these pages, that things such as honesty, peace, and virtue are good? And isn't it also true that you instinctively know, without anyone having to tell you, that things such as murder, lying, and stealing are bad and should be avoided?

That instinct you feel to love what is good and be repelled by what is bad is natural. It's human. It's God-given, because God is good, and He wants you to know the truth by which you can live and experience happiness and peace. Otherwise, if your instincts here were not God-given, how could you account for the fact that you know this to be true? How could you account for the fact that all human beings throughout history — people everywhere and at all times, regardless of their social or economic circumstances — know instinctively the very same thing? This doesn't mean that people always *obey* these moral truths they intuitively know to be true, but their failure to abide by that unwritten law of morality does not negate it.

When Jesus Christ commanded us to be good, kind, loving, just, merciful, patient, and forgiving, he was saying: *Live as God created you to live. Reflect His character of goodness and truth in your own actions. Be imitators of your Father in heaven.*

This is also why great thinkers like St. Thomas Aquinas could express these truths so succinctly, leading to the development of maxims such as *the proper object of the human intellect is the truth* and *the proper object of the human will is the good.*[22] Because God exists, and only because He exists, can believers speak of "truth" and "good." Without God, these concepts have no meaning apart from one's own personal preferences and whims.

Bottom line: The Christian theistic worldview can account for the real existence of a moral law, as well as humanity's universal recognition of that law. The Christian worldview provides the *preconditions* that make our experience in this essential issue of life intelligible.

> Morality isn't a minor part of our experience. It's at the heart of it.

Morality isn't a minor part of our experience. It's at the heart of it. God's existence as a personal and moral being and our creation in God's image — these are the preconditions that render our experience intelligible.

MATERIALIST MORALITY?

What about the naturalist worldview? Does it provide the preconditions that could make sense of our experience of morality? What exactly would right and wrong *be* if the naturalist or materialist worldview were true?

We've seen that atheists, for the most part, believe in a law of morality just like those who believe in God. And so we would want to ask our atheist friend: in a world in which nothing exists but material things, what is your basis for believing in the existence of right and wrong? What *are* right and wrong?

Ask yourself: Are right and wrong material "things"? Are they natural objects in the natural world like trees, bicycles, and sunflowers? If so, can you touch "rightness" or "wrongness"? How much do right and wrong weigh? Could one take right and wrong and hide them under the bed or in the kitchen pantry? Could a chemist mix up a batch of right and wrong? Could you feed "honesty" to your parrot?

And if right and wrong are not natural objects in the natural world, are they maybe natural properties — like the color yellow, or the property of smoothness?

Of course not. No one (atheists included) believes that realities such as honesty and goodness and right and wrong are properties like the color yellow. Yet, as we've seen, everyone everywhere (including atheists) knows that these "entities" are in some sense real and have an existence quite apart from the minds of the people who think about them. Right and wrong exist as standards above the mere preference and taste of cultures, societies, and individuals. And atheists cannot deny that they are universally perceived. But how can they adequately account for them according to their worldview, which insists that nothing exists except material "things"?

Could goodness and fairness and the laws of morality be non-material *moral* properties that exist in the real world alongside natural objects, but that attach to actions rather than objects? For instance, "It was *right* of you to keep your promise to your daughter." "It was *wrong* of you to cut into line ahead of that elderly woman who was there before you." "He *ought* to have treated his wife better." Could right and wrong be properties in this universe that are non-material, but real?

This is what believers say. And it makes sense for us to say this, because our worldview *includes* the existence of non-material — spiritual — entities, such as God, the human soul, and angels. But how could the atheist say this when he has already committed himself to a worldview whose essential belief is that "whatever exists or happens is natural" and that "the real world consists only of material things"? Since non-material "things" do not exist in a wholly natural universe, atheists have no basis to condemn lying, thievery, or murder.[23] In which case lies, theft, and murder are just as natural as anything else.

See the problem with this?

The Atheist's Moral Dilemma

Talking about non-material moral properties as existing in a naturalist universe is like talking about squares being seen scattered about in a universe of triangles, or symphonies being heard every Friday night in a world without sound.

This is what we mean when we say that the worldview we hold must be able to *account* for the view we have of morality.

In *Does God Exist?*, J. P. Moreland discusses this same issue. He points out that when we say, "Red is a color" or "This ball is red," we are saying something about the way the world is. Namely, we are committing ourselves to the idea that "certain entities" exist in the real world — in this case, "red," "color," and "ball." Likewise, when we say, "Kindness is a virtue," we mean that kindness and virtue are entities that exist in the real world.

> Just as the statement, "red is a color," commits one to believing in the existence of red and color, to say, "kindness is a virtue," commits one to believing in the existence of kindness and virtue.

Moreland then asks the question that goes to the heart of the matter:

> Now the question for any view regarding the nature and justification of morality is this: Is that view adequate, and if so, what general metaphysical worldview must we embrace to render intelligible a particular conception of morality.[24]

This is precisely the question atheists must confront: What view of the nature of the real world must one embrace in order to "render intelligible" one's concept of morality? For instance, if one believes that stealing is wrong, what view must one hold in order to *account* for the existence of a moral law against theft?

What are right and wrong in *this kind* of universe? If they are not material objects, are not natural properties, and cannot even be said to be non-material properties, then what are they?

We must challenge atheists to answer that unanswerable question. The simple truth is that there is absolutely no basis for anything like a moral *law* in a universe in which *nothing exists* but material substances. The preconditions for moral law simply do not exist in the naturalist worldview. There is no way to account for them.

In the end, to be consistent with what he has said to be true about the real world in which we live, the atheist must say that right and wrong *do not really exist,* and that they are *merely words individuals and societies have adapted to express their preferences.*[25]

In his book *Farewell to God,* Christian-turned-atheist Charles Templeton spends 21 pages cataloging in painful detail a wide range of evil "horrors" in this world — crime, disease, war, natural disasters, etc. — yet he never confronts, because he most likely does not even realize, the radical incoherence of his position. On the one hand, he vigorously denies the existence of God; on the other hand, he admits, "'Good' and 'evil' . . . are each inevitably, inescapably part of the way life is."[26]

Consider, for example, the view of the late J. L. Mackie, one of the most famous atheists of the late twentieth century. This is what he said about the possibility of right and wrong existing as non-material moral properties:

> Moral properties constitute so odd a cluster of properties and relations that they are most unlikely to have arisen in the ordinary course of events without an all-powerful god to create them.[27]

J. P. Moreland explains how Mackie, a committed philosophical atheist, sought to resolve this problem:

> Mackie's solution is to just deny the existence of these properties. And he goes on to argue that all we can do is create values subjectively; you just have to choose what you want to be.[28]

Now, while most atheists will usually want to stop short of this radical conclusion, the more consistent have been willing to accept the logical implications of their worldview.

And what *are* the logical implications of the naturalist worldview for morality? They are, simply, that right and wrong have no real existence; that there is no objective standard in this natural universe by which to judge the morality of an individual or society or civilization; that ethics are, therefore, personal and relative; that men and women, families and nations must simply choose for themselves what they will consider "right for them" and "wrong for them."

But the truth is even worse than this. The already sticky predicament in which the atheist finds himself gets much more problematic, as we will see next.

CHAPTER FOUR

THE BITTER FRUIT OF ATHEIST AMORALITY

Ideas govern the world or throw it into chaos.

— Auguste Comte

THUS SPAKE NIETSZCHE

Friedrich Nietzsche (1844-1900) has been often spoken of as the father of modern atheism. His own father was a Lutheran minister, his mother a devout Christian. Both of his grandfathers were ministers as well. Nietzsche intended to become a minister himself and traveled to Bonn to study theology at the university.

Over time, he came to believe that a crossroads in the evolution of Western civilization was reached in the nineteenth century. In academic circles, naturalism replaced Christian theism that had reigned for many centuries. Men no longer believed in the teachings of Christianity: God, the immortality of the soul, sin, grace, salvation, and eternal life. Christianity, Nietzsche felt, had been finally unmasked as a fraud and illusion.

Nietzsche came to reject Christianity and the very existence of God. And he came to see as well that atheism implied not only the relativity of the moral law but also the death of morality.

In his best-known work, *Thus Spake Zarathustra*, Nietzsche laid out his worldview. The main character, Zarathustra, goes to live on a mountain and work out his philosophy of the ideal world. Finally, he realizes that there is no God and that morality is an illusion. He heads down the mountain to inform the world of his discovery that Christianity and, indeed, all religions are a farce. Along the way, he meets a monk who has sacrificed everything for the love of God. The monk asks Zarathustra where he's going. He replies that he's going to shatter the delusions and myths that men and women live under — the myths of God and morality and religion. The monk pleads with him not to do this. As Zarathustra leaves he whispers to himself, "Has no one told him that God is dead?"

As Zarathustra enters the town, he immediately begins to preach the "good news" that God is dead and that man is at last freed from the enslaving bonds of Christian morality. The essence of his message was the essence of Nietzsche's worldview:

> Man is a rope, stretched between the animal and the Superman — a rope over the abyss. A dangerous crossing, a dangerous wayfaring, a dangerous looking back, a dangerous trembling and halting. . . . Ye have made your way from the worm to man, and much within you is still worm. Once were ye apes, and even yet man is more of an ape than any of the apes. . . . Believe not those who speak unto you of super-earthly hopes! Poisoners are they, whether they know it or not. Despisers of life are they, decaying ones and poisoned ones themselves,

of whom the earth is weary. Away with them!
Once blasphemy against God was the greatest
blasphemy; but God died, and therewith also those
blasphemers.[29]

According to Nietzsche, man is an animal evolving
from beast to what he referred to as the "superman" — a
race of men and women unchained from the shackles of
religion, belief in God, and morality, who will use their
intelligence and *will* to create their own world — any
world they like.

In the meantime, whatever stands in the way of this
evolution must be obliterated. More than anything else,
Christianity stands in the way, especially with its teachings
about humility and compassion, ideals that Nietzsche
detested. How, he asked, can man act in freedom while
weighted down with these chains? How can he erect a
civilization of power on pathetic ideals about love, peace,
and kindness to the "least of these"? Christianity must be
ruthlessly destroyed in order to make way for the race of
supermen who would rise above Christian superstition
about a God who isn't there.

Nietzsche's famous dictum "God is dead" summed up
his philosophical project. If God is dead, then with that
demise comes the death of any moral *law*. No God means
no right and wrong. "My basic law," he once wrote, is that
"there are no ethical phenomena . . ."

Once Nietzsche's worldview began to seep into the
European intellectual milieu, things started heading
downhill rapidly. The German atheist's views, combined

with ideas drawn from Darwin and other naturalist sources, were instrumental in propelling Europe — Germany in particular — toward the worst era of violence and brutality it had ever experienced.

NIETSZCHE'S DEVOTED DISCIPLE

One of Nietzsche's twentieth-century disciples was the failed Austrian artist, Adolf Hitler. Now, much nonsense has been written about Hitler being a Christian, believing in God, and opposing atheism.

But whatever this madman said at times in order to gain the confidence of the German people — who were at least culturally Christian — Hitler was clearly committed to a vision of the world that was essentially Darwinian and Nietzschean.

He was an admirer of Nietzsche. He read Nietzsche. He visited the Weimar Nietzsche archives in Berlin, where a photo was taken of him gazing at a bust of the great German philosopher. He had his own twisted version of Nietzsche's "superman" — the infamous Aryan master race. In his article *Was Hitler a Christian?*, Dinesh D'Souza comments that Nietzsche's concept of the "will to power" "almost became a Nazi recruitment slogan."[30] Hitler quite obviously despised, as did his atheist mentor, the core moral values of Christianity — goodness, mercy, love, and forgiveness, especially toward the "least." Instead, he worshipped the gods of power and lived by a morality that was akin to Nietzsche's new ethic for a new age "beyond good and evil." One Nazi academic wrote,

"When we call out to this youth, marching under the swastika: *'Heil Hitler!'* — at the same time we greet with this call: 'Friedrich Neitzsche!'"[31]

Hitler was no Christian. Rather, he saw himself as implementing a Darwinian "law of nature" that would result in the "elimination of the unfit" and bring about a civilization fit for a master race. In the execution of his project, Hitler understood with chilling clarity the moral implications of a Nietzschean world without God. And once he had risen to rule over Germany and much of Europe, and had amassed sufficient power, he *acted* on those principles. At the Auschwitz and Birkenau concentration camps, one can see on display the artifacts and evidences of Hitler's chosen morality.

> Much nonsense has been written about Hitler being a Christian, believing in God, and opposing atheism.

In his book *Can Man Live Without God?*, Protestant philosopher and author Ravi Zacharias describes a visit he made there:

> A few years ago when I was speaking in Poland I was taken to the Nazi death camps of Auschwitz and Birkenau. I shall never be the same. . . .
>
> On display for all to behold are thousands of pounds of women's hair, retrieved and marketed as a commodity by the Nazi exterminators, architects of the final solution that sent multitudes to the gas ovens. The incredible reminders — from rooms filled with pictures of abused and castrated children to the toiletries and clothing that are stacked to the

ceiling — cast an overwhelming pall of somberness on the visitor.[32]

Zacharias then asks the question: "Is there an explanation for Auschwitz, this mind-boggling historical scar on the face of humanity?" He believes there is an explanation and he finds it in the words of a Viktor Frankl, the famous Jewish psychologist, who survived the Nazi death camps:

> If we present man with a concept of man which is not true, we may well corrupt him. When we present him as an automation of reflexes, as a mind machine, as a bundle of instincts, as a pawn of drive and reactions, as a mere project of heredity and environment, we see the nihilism to which modern man is, in any case, prone. I became acquainted with the last stage of corruption in my second concentration camp, Auschwitz. The gas chambers of Auschwitz were the ultimate consequence of the theory that man is nothing but the product of heredity and environment — or, as the Nazis like to say, "of blood and soil." I am absolutely convinced that the gas chambers of Auschwitz, Treblinka, and Maidanek were ultimately prepared not in some ministry or other in Berlin, but rather at the desks and in the lecture halls of nihilistic scientists and philosophers.[33]

"Ideas govern the world or throw it into chaos,"[34] wrote Auguste Comte. Oh, how true that is.

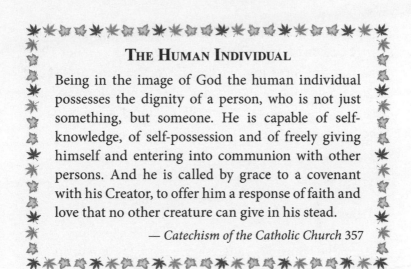

THE HUMAN INDIVIDUAL

Being in the image of God the human individual possesses the dignity of a person, who is not just something, but someone. He is capable of self-knowledge, of self-possession and of freely giving himself and entering into communion with other persons. And he is called by grace to a covenant with his Creator, to offer him a response of faith and love that no other creature can give in his stead.

— *Catechism of the Catholic Church* 357

DEADLY DEMAGOGUES

Yet another man committed to the dream of a civilization of power set free from the infantile constraints of belief in God was a Russian politician named Joseph Dzhugashvili. Like Nietzsche, in his early life Joseph had been a seminary student preparing for ministry in the Russian Orthodox Church. He eventually came to reject God and all religion as the mere invention of man, then went on to build one of the first officially atheistic states in the history of the world. Because of the force of his will, he came to be called *Stalin*, which means "steel" in Ukrainian.

In the Communist Party Archives in Moscow there is now a copy of Trotsky's *Terror and Communism* (1920), taken from Stalin's home after his death. Whenever in this work Trotsky praises revolutionary violence, one can see Stalin's handwritten comments of hearty approval scrawled in the margins: "Right!" "Well said!" "Yes!"[35]

In his book *Stalin,* Edvard Radzinsky describes how shortly before Stalin's fiftieth birthday, in December 1929, he had written an article in which he "defined the task ahead as 'the liquidation of the *kulak* [land-owning farmers] as a class.'" He chose January 1, 1930, to launch what he called "The Year of the Great Turn." Radvinsky writes:

> While he was celebrating the New Year with his family, his humiliated foes, and his servile henchmen, preparations were being made out on the boundless frozen expanses of Russia. Special freight cars stood ready on the rail tracks. Previously used to transport cattle, they were waiting now to transport human beings. . . . All over the country, as women howled and sobbed, the unfortunates were loaded into carts, which moved out of the villages under the watchful eye of the GPU (State Political Administration). People gazed round at the empty houses which had been their family homes for centuries.[36]

Radzinsky also describes the bloody purges that were a common feature of Stalin's rule:

> There was no shortage of people to shoot. Trucks kept their engines running at night to drown out the noise of shots and the screams. Bodies were stuffed into sacks and buried by moonlight. When day dawned, the relatives of the dead swarmed round the communal graves, digging up the fresh earth to find their loved ones for reburial.[37]

Stalin probably was personally responsible for the deaths of more innocent human beings than anyone who has ever lived. In the forced famines of 1932 and 1933 alone, engineered to bring about the collectivization of Russian farming, it is estimated that he purposely starved to death some seven million *kulaks*. Millions more were executed or taken to the gulags.

> Stalin probably was personally responsible for the deaths of more innocent human beings than anyone who has ever lived.

Two more bloody examples of the Godless delusion in action will suffice to make our point that atheists have used their amoral principles to wreak unthinkable violence against their fellow human beings around the world.

Mao Tse-Tung, the infamous Communist Chinese dictator, was a committed atheist — so committed, in fact, that he exerted the considerable might of the Chinese army and political apparatus to force, as far as he possibly could, all Chinese citizens under his regime into atheism. In Mao's China, every conceivable outrage that can be perpetrated against a human being was done, and on a scale that is practically impossible to fathom.

Jung Chang and Jon Halliday's book *Mao: The Unknown Story* begins with one of the most chilling sentences ever written:

> Mao Tse-Tung, who for decades held absolute power over the lives of a quarter of the world's population, was responsible for well over 70 million deaths in peacetime.[38]

In Cambodia, under the dictator Pol Pot's Khmer Rouge regime, more than two million human beings —

a third of the population — were executed or worked to death by their atheist guards acting under orders from their atheist boss. In the capital city, Phnom Penh, there is a girls' school building that, between 1975 and 1979, became an infamous prison. It is now a museum where one can still see the iron bed frames on which inmates were tortured, as well as the photos of thousands of men, women, and even children who were imprisoned there.

Only eight made it out alive.

A short distance outside the city lie the "killing fields." Some several hundred mass graves were located there; only twenty-nine of them have been excavated, but the results of that excavation are still stunning: a glass tower, some thirty feet high, filled to the top with human skulls. Walking around the site one can still see, protruding from the ground, bits of clothing not fully buried.

We believe it would be dishonest — even absurd — to suggest that what these atheists were able to do, their totalitarian policies and their mass slaughter of human beings, had no connection with their materialistic worldviews. Although atheism need not necessarily result in immorality and violence, it certainly leads some adherents in that direction. It removes from consideration the existence of a good and loving God — and with Him, any objective standard by which the actions or moral choices of another can be judged.

Good Atheists, Bad Christians

Upon saying such things, we immediately hear objections: "This isn't right! (There's that word "right" again. . . .) I know atheists who are good and moral people! And I know Christians who are not. And what about all the killing that has been done in the name of Christ?"

Let's be clear about what we're saying and what we're not saying: Our argument is *not* that atheists, as individuals, are all hideously immoral people, as the members of the rogues' gallery of mass-murders we just mentioned undeniably were. In fact, our argument has been exactly the reverse: that because atheists have been created in the image and likeness of God and know as well as believers that right and wrong exist, they demonstrate this in the way they live, despite their atheism.

The majority of atheists, no doubt, are men and women with high moral standards. Likewise, there have been plenty of believers in God who have behaved immorally.

> Many Christians treat other human beings as though they were animals, abusing them cruelly; many lie, steal, and murder.

There is no excuse for their sins. And, yes, there have been numerous instances of Christian institutions that have committed the same evil acts against human beings. But when they do, they are acting in a manner that is *inconsistent* with the Christian worldview that commands us to love one another and to treat others as having intrinsic value.

We aren't arguing that all or even most atheists are "bad people." Our argument, rather, is that *atheism,* as a *worldview* that cannot account for moral absolutes, teaches us that right and wrong are a matter of subjective personal opinion — entirely relative — and thus, gives us no reason not to treat others as means to our ends. In essence, the naturalist worldview doesn't teach us to be good.

In the atheist worldview of nature, it's good for the strong to devour the weak, because that is how the evolution of species progresses. And if human beings are nothing but — as one teacher of Christian apologetics put it — "the forward edge of the sludge of evolution," mere accidents of chance and time, material substances and nothing more, why *shouldn't* Hitler eliminate those he perceives to be the inferior weak? Assuming the truth of atheism, how do we know he wasn't helping to further the evolutionary advancement of the human species? Why *shouldn't* Stalin have liquidated those who stood in the way of his envisioned worker's paradise? He regarded human beings as animals and nothing more. All of this heinous slaughter follows — not necessarily, but consistently — from the naturalist worldview; in the pursuit of power and the ideal state, the individual was simply unimportant.

In short, Auschwitz, the forced famines, the killing fields — these were all, to use Zacharias's phrase, "atheism's legitimate offspring." Hitler, Stalin, and Mao were able to harden their hearts to the cries of children, young men and women, the elderly, the crippled — those unwanted for whatever reason. How were they able to do such a thing? Because they viewed these human beings as the mere "product of evolution." These men also had other issues to take into consideration: the health and happiness of the State, the State's ability to clothe and feed them, and other equally reasonable concerns.

How can anything be "wrong" if God does not exist and there is no moral law? We may not like what some have done. We may be appalled by it. But how can it be "wrong"?

As Dostoevsky famously said in *The Brothers Karamazov*, "If God does not exist, everything is permissible."

EVIL AND THE EXISTENCE OF GOD

In light of these crimes against humanity, it's interesting to hear atheists hold out the existence of evil as a key argument against the existence of God. You know how the argument goes: If an all-good and all-powerful God existed, then he would not allow evil to exist. Because evil does exist, an all-good and all-powerful God must not exist.

Now, this classic argument for atheism — an argument many believe to be the single most powerful refutation of the existence of God — can be dismantled on two levels.

First, this assertion is an unsound deductive argument. It's unsound because it assumes the truth of a premise that cannot be known. It takes for granted that an all-good and all-powerful God *could not* or *would not* allow evil to exist even for a limited time. And since evil does exist, the God Christians and others believe in cannot exist. Well, if it's true that an all-good and all-powerful God *could not* or *would not* allow evil to exist even for a limited period of time, then, of course, the argument works.

But how does the atheist know that an all-good and all-powerful God could have *no possible reason* for allowing evil to exist for a time? Of course, he cannot know this. In fact, a good, loving, and all-powerful God might conceivably have *a number of reasons* for allowing evil to exist for a time — and, apparently, He does.

It may be hard for us to understand why God allows evil, but the existence of evil does not prove the non-existence of God.

But on a deeper, more profound level, the so-called "problem of evil" becomes a problem not for the believer but for the atheist. The argument twists and turns to fall on the head of the one attempting to make it by actually arguing strongly *for* the existence of God. Ironically, it's only on the basis of a theistic worldview, in which God exists and provides an objective moral standard, that we can call anything objectively "evil."

Richard Dawkins, for example, attempts to make the argument from evil. This evangelist for atheistic naturalism presents the "problem of evil" in traditional fashion to disprove the existence of an all-good, all-powerful God.[39] But for all his attempts, neither he nor any atheist can really speak about "good" and "evil," if they are to be consistent. For if there is no supreme standard of "good," which would be God, then nothing can be rightly called "good" or "evil." Everything just *is*. And, therefore, any given human act, such as murdering an old woman for the money in her purse, or starving homosexuals, amputees, or mentally ill people to death because they are inconvenient to have around,[40] cannot really be classified as "evil." You may not like those actions — but if God does not exist, you have no basis higher than your own private preferences for labeling them as "evil" or demanding that other people not do those things.

Dawkins may want to use the existence of evil as an argument against the existence of the Christian God, but in a naturalist universe, evil doesn't even exist. In a naturalist

> Ironically, it's only on the basis of a theistic worldview, in which God exists and provides an objective moral standard, that we can call anything objectively "evil."

universe, nothing exists but particular material "things," simply doing what they naturally do.

And therefore, it turns out that the so-called "problem of evil" can be a problem only *within* a theistic worldview. *Within* a theistic worldview, one might legitimately ask the question: "Since God is all-good and all-powerful, I wonder why He allows evil to exist as He does, or to exist as long as He has? I wonder what God's purpose is in this?" A number of answers to this question can be pondered.

But the atheist? The naturalist? Men like Dawkins and Hitchens? These have to *assume* the existence of God and of moral absolutes (in other words, the truth of a worldview very much like the Christian theistic worldview) in order to *even pose the problem*. How then can the problem of evil be used as an argument *against* God's existence?

Atheists are, in a certain sense, like little children. Sometimes a child gets mad at her daddy and, without stopping to think about what she's doing, in her pique reaches up to slap her daddy in the face. Of course, she's too small to reach that high. In order to hit her father in the face, she has to first sit on his lap. Once he picks her up and sits her down on his lap, then she can smack him.

That's how it is for the atheist wanting to raise the problem of evil: He has to sit on God's lap before he can slap God in the face.

CHAPTER FIVE

THE ARBITRARY ETHICS OF ATHEISM

It's wrong, God or no God, to torture little children just for the fun of it. What basis we have for making this confident moral claim is another thing, but we know, if we know anything, if we have any moral understanding at all, that that is wrong.

— Kai Nielsen

Most atheists are moral people, men and women concerned with right and wrong, justice and fairness, who wish to treat others as they would wish to be treated. Few of them fall to their knees and repent in sackcloth and ashes the moment you point out that their belief in right and wrong has no foundation in the naturalist worldview, however. Rather, they come up with other ways of explaining to themselves how atheism can be true and morality not become an utterly subjective free-for-all.

Atheists commonly say things such as, "We don't need God in order to have ethics. In a naturalist worldview, right and wrong are based on . . ." And then they proceed to describe some alternative source and standard for ethics. These function as objections to the argument we've been making, so we need to have a look at them.

ALTERNATIVE STANDARD #1: HAPPINESS

Some atheists will argue:

There doesn't have to be an objective moral law rooted in and reflecting the character of a God.

We can figure out for ourselves how to make wise, good, and ethical decisions. One way would be to ask ourselves, especially when facing difficult moral decisions, the simple question: what will bring the greatest happiness to the greatest number of people? What choice will result in the greatest total amount of happiness?[41]

Now, the first serious problem with this alternative ethical standard is this: it's not as though the "greatest total amount of happiness" can be simply measured in order to make even quasi-objective decisions based on the resulting number. There is no neutral ground from which such a calculation can be made.

An atheist will define "happiness" in terms of his naturalist worldview and the values that flow from it. A Christian will define happiness in terms of his theistic worldview and the values that flow from it. A materialistic naturalist (now using "materialistic" in the Madonna "Material Girl" sense) might argue for small families on the grounds that each child will have better clothing, more toys and vacations, and a more expensive education — and, therefore, more happiness. A Catholic might argue for large families on the grounds that each child will have more love and more sharing, more memories, less "spoiling" — and, therefore, more happiness . . . since happiness doesn't come from possessions.

But the point is: our worldviews *determine* our values and our ideas of where happiness is to be found. Happiness is not some measurable commodity that can be weighed objectively as a basis for making ethical decisions.

> Happiness is not some measurable commodity that can be weighed objectively as a basis for making ethical decisions.

This alternative ethical standard has another serious problem. Once the happiness of the individual is subordinated to the happiness of the group, nearly anything can be justified with regard to the individual.

For instance, a chilling letter to the editor by Wesley J. Smith appeared in the May 2002 issue of *First Things* Magazine. Smith commented on prominent bioethicist Peter Singer and his justification of infanticide. It is a devastating rebuttal of the atheist happiness standard:

> The first officially sanctioned infanticide in Germany occurred in 1939 after the father of a disabled baby, "Baby Knauer," wrote to Chancellor Hitler seeking permission to have his son euthanized. Hitler, believing the time was ripe to begin eradicating the "defectives," sent his physician, Dr. Karl Brandt, to inform Baby Knauer's doctors that there would be no legal consequence for killing the infant. This was done, so pleasing Hitler that he issued a secret directive, licensing doctors to kill disabled infants.
>
> In *The Nazi Doctors*, Robert J. Lifton quotes a 1973 interview in which the father of Baby Knauer recalled the reasons Brandt and Hitler agreed to the killing of his son:
>
> > He [Brandt} explained to me that the Führer had personally sent him, and that my son's case interested him very much. The Führer wanted

to explore the problem of people who had no future — whose [lives were] worthless. From then on, we wouldn't have to suffer from this terrible misfortune, because the Führer had granted us the mercy killing of our son. Later, we could have other children, handsome and healthy, of whom the Reich could be proud.

Peter Singer's philosophical rationale for infanticide is indistinguishable from that stated by Brandt to Baby Knauer's father. Writing in his book *Practical Ethics* about the rightness of killing a hemophiliac infant, Singer states:

When the death of a disabled infant will lead to the birth of another infant with better prospects for a happy life, the total amount of happiness will be greater if the disabled infant is killed. The loss of a happy life for the first infant is outweighed by the gain of a happier life for the second [even if not yet born]. Therefore, if killing the hemophiliac infant has no adverse effect on others, according to the total view, it would be right to kill him.

What a difference fifty years makes: Brandt was hanged after the Nuremberg Trials. Peter Singer holds a prestigious tenured chair in bio-ethics at Princeton University.[42]

You can see what might be thought justified if we decided we were going to determine right from wrong on the basis of what we imagine will result in the greatest "total amount of happiness." If what is important in moral reasoning is the total amount of happiness, then, obviously, the happiness of the individual becomes secondary. The individual is no longer an end in himself but has become a *means* to the happiness of the group.

Not a secure and comforting place to be.

But, of course, Singer might respond: "No, what I said was that if killing the hemophiliac infant *has no adverse effect on others*, according to the total view, it would be right to kill him."

This, however, only serves to drive home all the more forcefully the utter subjectivity and arbitrariness of the happiness standard. So now we can kill an innocent child, but only so long as it has no adverse effect on *others?* But why this arbitrary limitation? If killing the child is going to result in the greatest total amount of happiness, and if one human being can be made to experience "adverse effects" in the process (the innocent child who dies — death falling generally under the category of "adverse effects"!), then why can't others be made to suffer adverse effects for the greater total happiness — for instance, the mother and father, brothers and sisters, grandparents, other relatives?

Why can't six people be made unhappy if their unhappiness brings about a greater total amount of happiness for 100, or 50, or even just 12 others? Twelve is more than six, after all. For that matter, why can't the decision be made without the consent of the family, on the basis of the total amount of happiness that will accrue to society when it is relieved of the financial burden of the hemophiliac child, or low-IQ child, or poor child?

With respect to the individual, virtually *anything* could be (and has been!) justified on the grounds that it will result in the greatest total amount of happiness for the greatest number. While the weighing of happiness can certainly offer some guidance in group decisions that are not intrinsically moral in nature (shall we have pie this week or cake?), it's not a sound moral standard.

But, philosophically speaking, the most serious problem with this alternative ethical standard of happiness — as we shall see with *every* manmade moral standard trotted out to replace the Christian standard of an objective moral law — is that, based upon the naturalist worldview, there's no reason why anyone should want to follow it. Worse, it's even *inconsistent* with the naturist worldview.

How so? Because if there is no God and no moral law; if human beings are the mere products of natural processes, accidents of chance and time who have come from nowhere and are going nowhere; and if humans have a few fleeting years of existence and that's it, forever and ever; then, *why* should we *care* about what results in the greatest total amount of happiness? Why should we choose to allow this arbitrary standard to bind us in our freedom? Why shouldn't we do what we want? Why shouldn't we pick our own arbitrary standard, such as "right will be whatever makes *me* happy"?

Rationally speaking, then, the naturalist universe both renders the "happiness standard" completely arbitrary and reveals its inconsistency. It *contradicts* a worldview that teaches that the way of nature is for the strong to prey upon the weak. If the survival of the fittest is what drives evolution forward, why would one wish to hinder the glorious advent of Nietzsche's "Superman" by limiting his options through concern for the happiness of others?

ALTERNATIVE STANDARD #2: DO NO HARM

This alternative is particularly popular in a day when freedom from the moral law is the primary goal. It goes something like this: "In ethics, pretty much anything you choose to do is fine, so long as you're not hurting someone else."

This, for instance, is the ethic of sexual liberation. As long as it's between consenting adults (or teenagers, some will stipulate), you should be free to do whatever you like, with whomever you like, in whatever combinations you like, and in whatever circumstances you like, in or out of marriage — so long as no one is "hurt" by it. But, of course, this ethical standard bottoms out on the same series of jagged reefs as the happiness standard.

"Hurt," in this instance, is most often narrowly defined in terms of sexually transmitted disease or the dreaded unwanted pregnancy. But in reality, whether or not one is being "hurt" by engaging in the kinds of behaviors that could be defined as private and consensual depends on *the kind of world we live in*.

If human beings are nothing but highly evolved animals, as atheists claim, then it could be argued that no "harm" is done when people behave like animals. Since human beings are not spiritual beings, then a hedonistic lifestyle may adequately provide what you want out of life. Go for it. Do whatever your desires and appetites and addictions and fetishes compel you to do. Right?

Wrong.

If God exists, and He designed human sexuality to be expressed and find its meaning and fulfillment in the loving commitment of marriage, family, and a stable society, then unbridled sexual activity might just be precisely what Christianity has understood it to be for the past 2,000 years: a destructive activity that attacks human dignity and, in the end, inflicts profound and lasting emotional, spiritual, and physical wounds and scars.

In reality, *everyone is hurt* by the "do no harm" ethic. Those involved in sexual promiscuity, or in other immoral activities that might be considered entirely "private," are hurt because God made them for something so much higher and better. They degrade themselves when they fail to pursue their higher calling. Those who follow their example are hurt — especially the children, who assume that this must be a good way to live. Parents — who would never have wanted this for their sons or daughters — are hurt. Even society itself is hurt as its moral tenor is diminished by such behavior, even as its proponents claim they're not "hurting anyone else."

The vast majority of post-Christian men and women know in their hearts that modern sexual mores are not good. Much as they may accept the MTV and *Sex and the City* view of human sexuality, they still teach their daughters and granddaughters about Sleeping Beauty, Cinderella, Prince Charming, and love's first kiss.

This demonstrates that no matter what they *say* about sexual freedom, they still have hope for something higher — if not for themselves, then at least for their children. And no matter what they do in their private lives, they know that what is accepted as social progress is not a happy advancement but, in reality, a sad and soul-numbing decline from what they believed could exist when they were innocent.

As with atheism's "happiness standard," there are two hidden rocky shoals upon which this alternative ethical standard is positively dashed and destroyed. This alternative standard is also entirely arbitrary and inconsistent with the naturalist worldview.

> Much as the vast majority of post-Christian men and women may accept the MTV and *Sex and the City* view of human sexuality, they still teach their daughters about Sleeping Beauty, Cinderella, Prince Charming, and love's first kiss.

Some pointed questions for atheists: Do you see the "do no harm" standard existing anywhere in nature? Is this something the natural world teaches you? Didn't Darwin claim that, in nature, the strong prey upon the weak and only the fittest survive? Isn't this how things should be in this strictly material universe?

After all, Darwin claimed that the "survival of the fittest" is the undeniable basis upon which every species evolves, is improved, or is eliminated. As the poet Alfred Tennyson famously wrote, nature is "red in tooth and claw." Darwin suggests that fighting with, wounding, killing, and eating other creatures is simply "natural" and, in fact, essential to the evolutionary process. It is not "wrong" for a hungry crocodile to lunge out of a river, grab an unsuspecting baby gazelle by the throat, and eat it. Fair enough. Animals do what animals do. They are not, after all, rational creatures capable of understanding or abiding by morality.

So we must demand of atheists: *Why,* if human beings are merely more highly evolved animals, is it universally understood to be wrong for one human being to steal from, injure, or kill another human being? What is the rational basis to insert the notion of "right and wrong" into an atheist worldview? At best, this alternative ethical standard is just an expression of individual *preference*; the idea that we should limit our behavior to that which does not "hurt others" is purely arbitrary. It is just another form of relativism that, as others have described it, is an exercise in having one's feet "planted firmly in mid-air."

As we saw with the "happiness standard," the consistent atheist is forced to admit that the "do no harm" standard flatly contradicts the naturalist worldview that embraces Darwin's fundamental evolutionary principle of "survival of the fittest." Every organism scraps for survival, competing with any other organisms that vie with it for supremacy.

Darwin and other atheists tell us that we are the evolutionary result of natural selection in which the survival of the fittest is guaranteed *not* by being "nice" to competitors, but by overpowering weaker competitors. So how can an atheist complain about the fact that someone stole his new iPhone when he wasn't looking, or burned his house down out of revenge, or seduced and ran off with his wife?

Some readers, atheists included, may find it hard to believe that Darwin held views that not only challenged the "do no harm" standard, but also justified heinous crimes against humanity. Benjamin Wiker discusses these ramifications of Darwinian morality in the November 2001 issue of *First Things*. He quotes Darwin as saying that, in accordance with the laws of nature and the survival of the fittest, "The civilized races of man will almost certainly exterminate and replace throughout the world the savage races."

And where are these savage races to be found? Wiker explains that, in Darwin's view . . .

> . . . the European race will inevitability emerge as the distinct species "human being," and all the transitional forms — such as the gorilla, the Negro, and so on — will be extinct.

Quoting Darwin:

> The break [the distance between man and ape] will then be rendered wider, for it will intervene between man in a more civilized state, as we may hope. . . . the Caucasian, and some ape as low as a baboon, instead of as at present between the Negro or Australian and the gorilla.[43]

Wiker points out that, according to Darwin, *"Natural selection functions not only between races, but also among individuals within races."* In this struggle for survival, Darwin notes that there is a kind of ironic reversal at play in which the more savage races may in some ways do better than the civilized European races, hampered as they are by more developed concepts of human compassion and kindness toward the weak. This works against the survival of the fittest. The ideas and words could have been lifted from the sermons of Nietzsche's Zarathustra himself.

Finally, Wiker quotes Darwin saying something truly remarkable, hinting broadly at something we're not aware of Nietzsche ever having advocated — although Hitler most certainly did:

> We civilized men . . . do our utmost to check the process of elimination [i.e. the elimination of human beings]; we build asylums for the imbecile, the maimed, and the sick; we institute poor laws; and our medical men exert their utmost skill to save the life of everyone to the last moment. . . . Thus the weak members of civilized societies propagate their kind. No one who has attended to the breeding of domestic animals will doubt that this must be highly injurious to the race of man . . . excepting in the case of man himself, hardly anyone is so ignorant as to allow his worst animals to breed.

But then, when economist Ben Stein points out in his film *Expelled: No Intelligence Allowed* that aspects of Darwinism led to Hitler and his eugenics program, the secular establishment roars: "This is outrageous! Darwin never said *anything* that could be taken as a justification for *anything* Hitler did!"

Like Darwin, the Marquis de Sade believed in the morality that derives from the survival of the fittest. De Sade was so infamous for his brutal treatment — including torture and murder — of women that the word "sadism" derives from his name. He once wrote:

> As nature has made us (the men) strongest, we can
> do with her (the woman) whatever we please.

Now, *that's* consistent with the atheist worldview . . . but certainly not the "do no harm" standard.

Ken illustrates this with the following story:

> Back in college, Tina (now my wife) and I used to talk about how we wanted to pull off a stunt in our biology class. We were too timid to carry it off, but the idea was good.
>
> We were going to have her walk into class early and take a front-row seat. Then about five minutes into the session, I was going to saunter in, walk up the center aisle, take Tina by the hair, throw her out of her seat and take her place. And then when the fireworks of moral outrage began, I was going to say, in mock astonishment, "Hey, hey! What's the problem? You've been teaching us that in the real world, the survival of the fittest reigns supreme. I'm obviously bigger than she is. Study after study has shown that students who sit in the front of the class do better academically than those who sit further back. Those who do better academically get the best jobs. Don't you want the strongest to succeed?"

How interesting (not to mention comical) it would have been to watch the biology instructor with the entire class, many of them naturalists and moral relativists, leap up in unison to insist that it is "wrong to hurt others."

So much for the "do no harm" ethic.

ALTERNATIVE STANDARD #3: MAJORITY RULE

According to this proposed ethical standard for a naturalist world, whatever the majority of people say is right, is right — for that culture, in that time.

This would be the ethic of the supposed Eskimo tribes who elect to send their elderly off to sea on blocks of ice — a moral choice to which, of course, they are perfectly entitled and about which we Eurocentrists — especially Americans — have no right to judge, or to question, or even to raise an eyebrow. According to this standard, morality is based on social consensus. This is the ethic of Kinsey and his infamous statistical sexual studies: "Do what the norms show is normal."

This ethical alternative fails in a number of ways.

First, it's simply preposterous. If majority opinion really was the best or even a passable method for determining morality within a given society, then right and wrong would change as often as majority opinion changed. In this case it would be best to implant a transmitter into each person's brain so that a continuous computerized consensus could be taken as the basis for ever-changing ethical norms. Imagine it:

> Dec. 3, 2009: According to a poll taken this morning, abortion is to be considered morally "right" by a margin of three percent.

> Jan. 14, 2010: Breaking news. A new book recently published and arguing persuasively the case against abortion has apparently shifted the consensus. As of last evening around 7:30 p.m. PST, abortion has become "wrong." The confirmed margin was two percent.

The essential problem with the majority-rule ethic is that it is arbitrary and inconsistent with the very worldview of those who would suggest it. Why would the Marquis de Sade care what the people within his society think? Why should he submit to democratic rule when he lives in a universe in which morality has no objective existence? Would it matter at all to him that 51 percent of the population doesn't want him torturing women?

> Would it matter at all to the Marquis de Sade that 51 percent of the population doesn't want him torturing women?

Patrick relates an experience he had with a moral relativist that illustrates the futility of this atheist approach:

> I was standing in the checkout line at a store some years ago and struck up a conversation with the person behind me. Somehow, I don't remember why, it came up that my wife and I have a lot of children (11, though I think, at the time of this incident, we had only 9).
>
> "*What*?" the 60-ish woman standing in front of me whirled around and demanded indignantly of me. "You have *how many* children?"
>
> "Nine," I said, nonplussed by her obstreperous reaction.
>
> "Why, that is the most terrible, *selfish* thing I've ever heard of! You should be ashamed of yourself!"
>
> "Selfish?" I asked her. "How is having a large family 'selfish'?" It had never occurred to me that the sacrifices associated with feeding, housing, and caring for a large family could ever be considered "selfish." After all, deferring (permanently, in most cases) personal desires for things like a boat, expensive vacations, nice cars, etc., in favor of spending one's hard-earned income on mundane things like groceries, clothes, shoes, medical

expenses, and college tuition on a rambunctious herd of growing children does not strike me as "selfish." (Ditto for other parentesque duties like getting up from a deep and satisfying sleep in the middle of the night to clean up one's vomit-covered child who's sick with the stomach flu, etc.)

"It's selfish because all those kids are taking up precious resources," she responded. "You're anti-abortion, I'll bet." She glared at me. "You and your large family are why I am pro-choice!"

"But, ma'am," I said, "abortion is wrong. It's the murder of an unborn child." At that, her already flaring nostrils flared even wider and her scowl deepened.

"Abortion is *legal*," she said acidly, jabbing her index finger in the air for emphasis. "Get over it."

"Get over what?" I asked.

"Abortion. It's legal. Get over it." And that is when I knew I had her.

"Are you saying that because abortion is legal, it is morally acceptable? It's good?"

"It wouldn't *be* legal if it weren't," she sneered, fixing me with a look reserved for a dolt who should know better than to ask such a stupid question.

"But Negro slavery used to be legal in the United States, before the Emancipation Proclamation," I reminded her. "Was slavery morally 'okay' just because it was legal?"

She continued to glare at me, arms folded firmly across her chest, saying nothing.

"And don't forget," I added, "It was legal in Germany in the 1940s for Hitler to round up and kill six million Jews during the Holocaust. Was *that* morally okay, just because it was 'legal'?"

By now, a vein in this woman's forehead was throbbing. Obviously, our conversation was about to come to a screeching stop. She looked like a volcano ready to blow. I played my last card:

"Until 1920, it was perfectly legal in the U.S. to deny women the right to vote. How would you have felt if, in 1915, I told you "Tough luck, lady. It's legal for us men to prevent you women from voting. It's legal. Get over it"?

She stalked off in a rage without another word. What else was there for either of us to say?

ALTERNATIVE STANDARD #4: THE EXPERTS

Some God-deniers (and a great many more who are influenced by their books) assure us:

> The average person[44] is just not qualified to decide these matters in a universe in which moral laws are essentially ours to create. We must let the experts in science, medicine, law, and education work out our ethical standards for us.

(The fact that the great majority of those propounding such a prejudiced view are *themselves* experts in science, medicine, law, and education is, apparently, not supposed to give us pause.)

The "Let the Experts Decide Morality for Us" slogan is quite common nowadays, especially in the field of medicine — in particular, its subdiscipline of so-called "medical ethics."[45] This notion is absurd and frightening, when you stop to consider its sinister implications.

James D. Watson, the American Nobel Prize-winning molecular biologist,[46] seriously suggested that society should change the legal definition of "person" to apply only to infants *older than three days*. This would allow adequate time for someone to decide if a baby should be permitted to live. And Francis Crick, a famous biochemist and one of the discoverers of the structure of DNA, wrote an article titled "Why I Study Biology." In this article he answers the title's question:

> It is for philosophical and what you might call religious reasons. We all know, I think, or are beginning to realize, that the future is in our own hands, that we can, to some extent, do what we want.

Some of the things Dr. Crick, as well as others who think like him, have proposed at one time or another:

1. Design and program the type of future we want.
2. Begin thinking about genetically engineering the kind of people we want for society in the future.
3. Use medicine for goals other than humanitarian goals; medicine should not make the world safe for senility.
4. Structure society through who is *allowed*[47] to have children.
5. Indoctrinate the young to these goals starting at as early an age as possible.

There is no neutral base from which decisions about right and wrong are made on scientific grounds. The moral decisions of experts will be, to a great extent, determined by the worldviews they hold. An expert with a Christian theistic worldview will argue that abortion is harmful and wrong. An expert with a naturalist worldview will argue that it is right and useful. Letting "experts" determine right and wrong led to the eugenics movements in early twentieth-century America and Europe, culminating in the horrors of the Nazi experiments.

The goal of "genetically engineering the kind of people we want for society in the future" motivated death camp Dr. Josef Mengele, the "Angel of Death," to inject blue dye into the eyes of children and perform various surgeries on twins without anesthesia, including organ removal, castration, and amputations.

Given all this, how can we expect experts to decide?

> Letting "experts" determine right and wrong led to the eugenics movements in early twentieth-century America and Europe, culminating in the horrors of the Nazi experiments.

Some, such as Peter Singer, will no doubt apply the standard of whatever they imagine will result in the greatest total amount of "happiness" for the largest number of people. Other experts may insist that pretty much anything one chooses to do is fine, so long as you're not hurting someone else. Still others may want to consider majority opinion within a given society. But primarily, to decide these sensitive matters, experts will look to . . . well, other experts.

THE LIMITS OF SCIENCE

Science and technology are precious resources when placed at the service of man and promote his integral development for the benefit of all. By themselves, however, they cannot disclose the meaning of existence and of human progress.

It is an illusion to claim moral neutrality in scientific research and its applications. On the other hand, guiding principles cannot be inferred from simple technical efficiency, or from the usefulness accruing to some at the expense of others or, even worse, from prevailing ideologies. Science and technology by their very nature require unconditional respect for fundamental moral criteria. They must be at the service of the human person, of his inalienable rights, of his true and integral good, in conformity with the plan and the will of God.

— *Catechism of the Catholic Church* 2293; 2294

The bottom line is that, as an ethical standard, this criterion is as arbitrary and foundationless as the others. According to atheists, in their material universe in which right and wrong do not even exist, why in the world would anyone choose to allow scientific elites to determine ethics for him? If Darwin's atheistic assumption of "survival of the fittest" is true, then the experts should just shut up, sit down, and get out of the way so that everyone can decide for himself what's best, and thus, sink or swim in life's vast, meaningless swamp of natural selection.

ALTERNATIVE STANDARD #5: REASON

Some people will tell you:

> We don't need to believe in God in order to have morality. We can determine what is right and wrong by using our minds to think these issues through. Reason can be our guide in morality, as it is in everything else.[48]

Atheists claim that *their* model provides happiness for the greatest number of people. Pointing to societal and cultural consensus, various atheist experts in science, law, and education claim they merely seek to allow *reason* to rule in the realm of morality, rather than faith, religion, or opinions about what some "god" somewhere wants people to do and not do.

Immanuel Kant, the eighteenth-century German philosopher, is a hugely important figure in this regard. Many modern atheists look to Kant's works, such as *Critique of Pure Reason* and *Critique of Practical Reason*, as providing the rational foundation for the development of a purely naturalist morality.

Kant believed that right and wrong could be derived from, and ought to be based upon, reason alone. But he claimed that to avoid skepticism or nihilism, we must view morality as absolute and universal.

And so, Kant laid a foundation (at least in the minds of many of his atheist admirers) for a set of moral laws that are unlimited, universal, and unchanging, but which do not rely on the existence of God or divine revelation for their validity. He referred to these rules of morality as "categorical imperatives." Examples included "always tell the truth"; "always keep promises"; "be benevolent to those in need"; and "do not commit suicide."

In *Does God Exist*, atheist Kai Nielsen — in his debate with Christian philosopher J. P. Moreland — develops a modern variant of this position. He argues that even though a moral law does not exist in the natural world, just as we use our senses to gather information about the physical world, so we can use our best judgment to gather information upon which to make sound moral decisions.

For instance, Nielsen argues, it doesn't take God's existence for us to figure out what is just and fair in a given situation. Do we really need God in order to know that we ought to keep our promises, or tell the truth, or pay our debts, or allow an elderly woman to take our seat on the bus, or love our children? If we want to be treated with respect and dignity, isn't it only reasonable that we should treat others with respect and dignity? Certainly, we can perceive that human suffering is bad and that we ought to try to relieve it when we can — without God having to command us to do so! In other words, it doesn't take a genius — and it certainly doesn't take the existence of God — for us to figure out how we ought to conduct ourselves morally.

"Justice," Nielsen writes, "hardly requires God." In fact, he goes on to forcefully express this point of view:

> It's wrong, God or no God, to torture little children just for the fun of it. What basis we have for making this confident moral claim is another thing, but we know, if we know anything, if we have any moral understanding at all, that that is wrong.[49]

Of course, what *basis* Nielsen has for making this confident claim is an important question. At one point, he anticipates the objection that he has no metaphysical foundation for his moral point of view.

> Yeah, so, Nielsen, you affirm all those things. You give expression to your deep moral commitment, but you, the bloody secularist that you are, need to explain to us on what basis, what foundation, do you make these affirmations. Aren't these just your personal preferences? What foundations do you have?[50]

Note carefully his answer:

> Well, I would say . . . that they rest on my considered judgments that I can fit into what I call wide reflective equilibrium. . . . Just as sensory experience is to science, so in morality we start with considered judgments or, if you will, intuitions. . . . And then you try to get them into a coherent pattern with everything else you know, with the best theories of the function of morality in society, with the best theories we have about human nature, and so forth and so on. . . . [Your moral judgments] are justified by putting them into a coherent pattern. . . . [T]hat's as much — indeed it's the only kind — of objectivity I think you can get in ethics.[51]

This notion of morality as founded upon reason — or "wide reflective equilibrium," or whatever we decide to call it — entails two distinct issues that proponents blend into one, creating much confusion. First, there is the issue of what worldview can provide a *basis* for our belief in the objective existence of right and wrong. As we have seen, while the Christian worldview can provide this basis, the naturalist worldview cannot.

Catholic philosophers Peter Kreeft and Ronald Tacelli explain the atheist's morality predicament:

> Real moral obligation is a fact. We are really, truly, objectively obligated to do good and avoid evil. Either the atheistic view of reality is correct or the "religious" one. But the atheistic one is incompatible with there being moral obligation. Therefore the "religious" view of reality is correct. . . .
>
> Suppose we say [morality] is rooted in nothing deeper than human willing and desire [as atheists commonly do]. In that case, we have no moral standard against which human desires can be judged. For every desire will spring from the same ultimate source — purposeless, pitiless matter. And what becomes of obligation? According to this view, if I say there is an obligation to feed the hungry, I would be stating a fact about my wants and desires and nothing else. I would be saying that I want the hungry to be fed, and that I choose to act on that desire. But this amounts to an admission that neither I nor anyone else is really obliged to feed the hungry — that, in fact, no one has any real obligations at all. Therefore, the atheistic view of reality is not compatible with there being genuine moral obligation.
>
> What view is compatible? One that sees real moral obligation as grounded in its Creator, that sees moral obligation as rooted in the fact that we have been created with a purpose and for an end. We may call this view, with deliberate generality, "the religious

view." But however general the view, reflection on the fact of moral obligation does seem to confirm it.[52]

Second, atheism must grapple with the question of how we come to *know* this moral law and to *determine* right from wrong. Can right and wrong come to be known by reason alone, or do we need God to tell us?

This is a metaphysical question — that is, a question about the nature of reality with respect to the existence of right and wrong. It is also an epistemological question — that is, a question about how we come to know right from wrong. Atheists who look to Kant seem to forget that he personally believed in God and understood His existence to be interwoven with his own innate sense of morality.

The implications of this important detail about Kantian metaphysics and ethics are typically left unmentioned by atheists who seek to borrow from his philosophical system.

> Atheists who look to Kant seem to forget that he personally believed in God and understood His existence to be interwoven with his own innate sense of morality.

For example, it is unlikely that atheist purveyors of Kantian thought will draw your attention to this passage in *Critique of Pure Reason:*

> No one, no doubt, will be able to boast again that he *knows* that there is a God and a future life. For the man who knows that is the very man whom I have been so long in search of. . . . No, that conviction [i.e., that God exists] is not a *logical*, but a *moral* certainty; and, as it rests on subjective grounds (of the moral sentiment), I must not even say that *it is* morally certain that there is a God, etc.

> What I really mean is, that the belief in a God and
> in another world is so interwoven with my moral
> sentiment that as there is little danger of my losing
> the latter, there is quite as little fear lest I ever be
> deprived of the former.[53]

Kant believed in the existence of God. He understood that the *existence* of morality was rooted in God and is dependent on His existence. Because of this, he argued, human reason can discover right and wrong. Moral laws that we all instinctively recognize can be deduced by reason alone; therefore, they are *based on* reason.

Virtually all atheists understand that it makes no sense to argue for the existence of moral laws that are absolute, universal, and unchanging (as Kant did) in a universe comprised entirely of ever-changing and evolving material substances (which Kant denied). This is why most atheists will argue for the relativity of ethics from individual to individual and society to society.

This brings us to Kai Nielsen and his theory of "wide reflective equilibrium." Nielsen does not believe that moral truths are things that exist in the real world and that we *discover* through the use of reason. There are no moral facts in a naturalist universe; there is only the material world. And in this material world, we *create* morals as we engage in this process of "wide reflective equilibrium." As we observe the world, make judgments about how things are, test those judgments against other things we know, and fit them together into a coherent whole that makes sense, we are *creating values and ethics* for ourselves to live by. Each of us must choose how we are going to live. Nielsen has chosen to live a moral life.

Our fundamental critique of this point of view is identical to our critique of every alternative moral standard. As "reasonable" as it sounds, it is arbitrary and inconsistent with the naturalist worldview to say that reason will determine for us what is right and wrong.

It would be fair to say to the atheist:

> We agree with you, with Nielsen, and with Kant that we can come to *know* what is right and what is wrong by the use of reason alone. After all, the moral law exists and is reasonable. And God has written His moral law on our hearts and given us reason so that we might understand the world He has created. So, sure, we can come to know right and wrong through reason alone. However, our question to you is: in a universe such as you say we live in, why should we care to limit our choices by reason? Why not do what we like?

Atheists might say that living a certain way is "reasonable" — for instance, always telling the truth, always keeping promises, being benevolent to those in need, or not committing suicide. But if the *reality* is that there is no God and no moral law; if nothing exists but material substances; if man has evolved upwardly from the primordial soup of organic matter and is nothing more than an evolutionary accident; why should the notion of "reason" bind him to any particular type of conduct?

In the world of nature, whatever *exists* is natural — and whatever is natural, one could argue, is "right." So why not live in accordance with the laws we see operating in the physical world?

J. P. Moreland expresses this argument well:

> On an evolutionary secular scenario . . . Human beings are nothing special. . . . The same processes that coughed up human beings coughed up amoebas; there is nothing special about being human. The view that being human is special is guilty of specieism, an unjustifiable bias toward one's own species. The same process that coughed us up is eventually going to swallow us up, and in fact there is a good chance that we will evolve toward higher forms of life sometime in the future. There are no such things as non-natural properties or moral properties. Now the question that needs to be asked is this: In a universe of that sort, what possible reason could be given for why I should be moral? If [God does not exist] and there is no moral truth to be discovered and if I have to simply choose the moral point of view because that type of life is what I find worthwhile for myself, then the decision is arbitrary, rationally speaking. And the difference between, say, Mother Teresa and Hitler is roughly the same as the difference between whether I want to be a trumpet player or a baseball player.[54]

And so with the alternative ethical standard of reason, we wind up essentially where we wound up with all the others. Because the naturalist worldview cannot support the real existence of right and wrong, any standard of morality the atheist comes up with is going to be *ultimately arbitrary*. It will simply be his or her "idea" of a good way to have some semblance of morality in an immoral, impersonal, meaningless universe. Often, it will also be inconsistent and even contradictory to the naturalist worldview. To see this, all one has to do is ask the question: How exactly does this ethical standard arise naturally from an infinite sea of ever-changing material substances?

In every case the answer will be: It doesn't.

In a universe without God and without the real existence of right and wrong, moral codes based on measurements of total happiness, or ideas about what hurts others, or majority opinion, or the views of experts, or even reason, will always be a bit like traffic laws. The laws that instruct us, for instance, to drive on the right side of the road — these laws are fundamentally arbitrary. They are enacted not because there is anything intrinsically wrong in the moral sense with driving on the left side of a road (we hope not, for the sake of our friends on the British Isles!), but for purely practical purposes, so that the streets of our cities don't descend into utter chaos.

Ditto for ethical standards dreamed up in a naturalist universe: they are purely practical and fundamentally arbitrary.

LIFE WITHOUT GOD

In *Can Man Live Without God?* Ravi Zacharias writes:

> Time and again it was proven that it is not possible to establish a reasonable and coherent ethical theory without first establishing the *telos*, i.e. the purpose and destiny of human life. . . . If life itself is purposeless, ethics falls into disarray. . . . This, may

I suggest, is North America's predicament. This is
the albatross around our educator's necks. . . . We
continue to talk of values and ethics; we persist in
establishing moral boundaries for others while
erasing the lines that are drawn for life itself.

If I am merely the product of matter and at the
mercy of material determinism, why should I subject
myself to anyone else's moral convictions? If, on the
other hand, I am fashioned by God for His purpose,
then I need to know him and know that purpose for
which I have been made, for out of that purpose is
born my sense of right and wrong. There are two
worlds represented by these options.[55]

He's right. Two worlds. Two worldviews. One that *can*
make sense of morality and one that cannot.

Thus, the atheist lives in tension. He says one thing
and knows in his heart of hearts that another is true.

The atheist ethics professor teaches ethical relativism,
mocks Christianity with its moral absolutes, and explains
to his class that "right" and "wrong," as objective moral
standards, do not exist. But then he "absolutely" demands
that you not cheat on his test on ethical relativism. If you
do cheat, he immediately forgets that he's an atheist and
begins speaking like a Christian, insisting that "cheating
is wrong and you should know that!"

He can't help it. After all, he's in the image of God; no
matter what he says he believes about the world, he always
has to deal with what he is, and what he knows by virtue
of what he is.

Oh, by the way, this ethics professor — he'll become even more committed to the existence of the moral law if you just skip the test entirely, put a gun to his head and tell him, Stalin-style, to give you and A. "Or, make that an A+, thank you."

In conclusion, Ken tells the following story:

> I turned on the TV a few years back and there was Bill O'Reilly going absolutely insane. Some new study had apparently shown a dramatic increase in cheating among high school and college students. The young college student he had on as a guest repeatedly said that she saw nothing wrong with cheating if it was going to help her get ahead in a highly competitive professional world. O'Reilly was so frustrated being forced to defend what seemed perfectly self-evident to him — that cheating is wrong — that he couldn't formulate a response. In his flabbergasted state, unable to reason with the student, he cried out to another guest on his show, I believe a professor, of psychology, "Why is this happening? Doctor, you're the expert, explain what is going on!"
>
> I almost wanted to stand up and scream at the television: "Dostoevsky! If God does not exist, everything is permissible!"

We cannot teach people that they are nothing but material "things" that have evolved out of the slime and then try to also teach them that there is a moral law they need to abide by. They are too smart to not see the implications of the atheism they're taught. So they reason this world is a struggle for existence, and if cheating on a few tests will help me to get ahead and get the good job and earn the good money, then why not?

There is no foundation for morality apart from God. And if naturalists really began to live in a manner consistent with their worldview, their moral lives would implode.

We see some of this already.

Chapter Six

Atheism Eliminates Knowledge

The important point about the standard evolutionary story is that the human species and all of its features are the wholly physical outcome of a purely physical process. If this is the correct account of our origin, then there seems neither need nor room to fit any nonphysical substances or properties into our theoretical accounts of ourselves. We are creatures of matter.

— Paul Churchland

Frank J. Sheed, the renowned twentieth-century debater of atheists, recounts the following incident. During a public lecture on the Catholic faith in Liverpool, England, he was heckled by an atheist who "ended a long catalogue of what was wrong with the universe by saying, 'I could make a better universe than your God made.'" Sheed responded, "I won't ask you to make a universe. But would you make a rabbit, just to establish confidence?"[56]

Atheists are quite confident in their denial of God's existence, and they seek to explain everything around them, including human knowledge, as being the result of natural, physical processes. But as we will see in this chapter, atheism by its very nature cannot avoid the *reductio ad absurdum* of eliminating knowledge altogether. Rather than being "rational" and "fact-based," the naturalist worldview simply cannot account for reason, facts, and knowledge.

All the evidence — philosophical, scientific, existential, commonsense — points inexorably to the fact that only the worldview that posits the existence of God can fit our experience. Recognizing the existence of God enables us to account for everything science can teach us about the nature of the material world. It also makes it possible to account for what we all intuitively understand to be true about the most basic "non-material" issues of life, such as happiness, memory, morality, knowledge, human dignity, individual personality, love, meaning, and value.

On the other hand, naturalism does not describe the world as it really is. It fails miserably to make sense of the richness and meaning of human experience. And when it comes to dealing in particular with the fundamental human issues of morality, knowledge, or the intrinsic value of the human person, the atheist is — as one Christian apologist described him — like a man made of water attempting to climb out of an infinite ocean of water on a ladder made of water.

Much like a hapless man who is busily engaged in shoveling smoke or pushing rope upward, modern atheists expend a great deal of time and energy trying to account for knowledge based on a system that denies the Ultimate Knower, from Whom everything else that can be known comes.

In this chapter, we argue that God's existence alone provides the necessary metaphysical preconditions for knowledge. Remove God from the universe and you remove the possibility of knowledge with Him.

> Remove God from the universe and you remove the possibility of knowledge with Him.

We will argue that human reason itself presupposes the existence of God, such that, if naturalism were true, and God did not exist, no one could know anything at all — including the idea that naturalism is true. Sound a bit tricky? Don't worry. We'll show you how this works and how you can effectively explain to others this fatal flaw in atheism.

OF WORLDVIEWS AND IRON BEDS

Procrustes, a curious figure from Greek mythology, lived in a fortress on Mount Korydallos, on the road between Athens and Eleusis. When travelers made their way past his lair, Procrustes would invite them to join him for a pleasant meal and rest for the night. He had a special bed, he explained to each of his guests, one that they would surely want to try out — an iron bed that somehow matched exactly the length of every person who lay on it.

What Procrustes failed to mention was the unusual method by which this "one size fits all" miracle bed worked. As soon as he had his guest stretched out on the bed, he would make sure his guest fit his bed. Those who were too short, he would stretch on the rack to make them longer. Those who were too tall, he would cut down to size, amputating as much of their legs as was required to achieve a perfect length. In the end, everyone fit the bed. Procrustes made sure of it. (Not a coincidence, then, that his name in Greek means "he who stretches.")

It wouldn't be much of a stretch (if you will forgive the pun) to say that Procrustes was the ultimate reductionist. And, in one way or another, the terrible things Procrustes did to his guests, all reductionist worldviews do to human experience. Stretching a bit here and whittling down a bit there, the reductionist worldview forces human experience to fit a preconceived vision of reality as reducible to one essential thing: Matter — material "things" such as particles, atoms, quarks, strings, whatever the most basic "stuff" turns out to be — is all there is. No spirit. No God.

Then, some unenlightened Christian furrows his brow at this claim and says:

> But it sure doesn't *seem* like everything is matter. I mean, what about right and wrong? Are these material things? What about love? What about ideas? What about knowledge and reason and the process of thinking? These are not material things or "material processes."

Presented with these questions, however, the naturalist assures the poor deluded Christian that although these may not *seem* to be material things, each of them is in some way reducible to matter — either that, or they simply don't exist.

In the previous chapters, we witnessed the destruction of morality as it was chopped down to create the required "fit" with a naturalist/atheist view: what lay down in the evening as moral law arose in the morning as mere personal preference. In this chapter, we will show that knowledge and truth fare even worse than morality when placed on the Procrustean bed of atheist naturalism.

THE MIRACLE OF THE MIND

Ken tells this story:

When my son Kenny was little, he listened endlessly to Disney sing-along tapes. There were four of five of these I would hear playing around the house so often I thought I would lose my mind. There was one song in particular that used to drive me up the wall. The chorus went like this:

You are a human animal
You are a very special breed
For you are the only animal
Who can think, who can reason, who can read.

Much of what Disney does is geared toward children, most of whom are being raised in families that believe in God. Although their stories are filled with fairy godmothers and magical princesses, when they address a scientific subject they consistently take a naturalistic view. I remember thinking when I would hear that song, "These people at Disney have no idea just how special a breed we are. If naturalism were true, they wouldn't be able to think about it, much less talk and compose songs about it!"

And that's a key question we want to ask in this chapter: If naturalism were true, would we be able to write songs about it?

Think about the miracle of the mind. Not only are we human beings able, through our senses, to take in impressions of the material world — images, sounds, smells, tastes, textures — but we are able to sort out these impressions, organize them, and abstract from them ideas and concepts. And not just simple concepts or ideas such as the concept of a square, but unbelievably complicated ideas, like imaginary numbers, or general relativity, or the curvature of time and space . . . or even the idea that God's existence alone can account for moral absolutes.

Even small children reason inductively from sets of facts and work with simple probability equations ("Mommy gave me candy yesterday and the day before; chances are she will give me candy today"). They reason deductively, drawing logical (if not always correct) conclusions from sets of premises ("My daddy watches college football; my daddy is a man; therefore all men watch college football"). As their minds mature, many will develop the ability to work through unbelievably lengthy logical and mathematical proofs, even though they will have never seen the simplest example of one in the natural world.

> Even small children reason inductively from sets of facts and work with simple probability equations ("Mommy gave me candy yesterday and the day before; chances are she will give me candy today").

With our minds, we think, we reason, we desire, we dream, we remember, we intend, we wonder, we believe, we love, we deceive, we doubt, we create humor, and we develop and use language to communicate all of this to one another.

We *are* a very special breed, indeed.

But how do we *account* for these abilities? Did the abilities described here evolve randomly from non-thinking material substances? How can love, doubt, happiness, and honesty be material things? How could individual consciousness arise from brute matter?

MAN IS RATIONAL AND LIKE GOD

The human person participates in the light and power of the divine Spirit. By his reason, he is capable of understanding the order of things established by the Creator.

God created man a rational being, conferring on him the dignity of a person who can initiate and control his own actions.

"God willed that man should be 'left in the hand of his own counsel,' so that he might of his own accord seek his Creator and freely attain his full and blessed perfection by cleaving to him."* "Man is rational and therefore like God; he is created with free will and and is master of his own acts."** (*Gaudium et Spes*, 17; Sirach 15:14; **St. Irenaeus, *Adv. Haeres.* 4,4,3:PG 7/1, 983)

— *Catechism of the Catholic Church* 1704; 1730

CAN MATTER THINK?

One of the most brilliant and well-known abstract thinkers of our time is Stephen Hawking. In 1988, he published *A Brief History of Time*. Something under 10,000 copies were initially printed — after all, this is not the kind of book that sells like a Harry Potter novel. But in one of the most remarkable surprises of publishing history, the book was an instant hit worldwide. It wound up staying 237 weeks on the (UK) *Sunday Times* best-sellers list, shattering all existing records, and has through the years sold over 9 million copies.

Nine million copies of a book elucidating the basics of relativity theory and quantum mechanics!

There should be little doubt that the near-miraculous response this book has received cannot be explained by its content, which most purchasers have probably not even understood. Rather, the near-miraculous life of the man who wrote the book accounts for its success. For one cannot look at Stephen Hawking without being moved, inspired, and reminded of a miracle that far exceeds all publishing miracles — the miracle of the human person and of the human mind.

Hawking was born in 1942. As a young man, he completed his degree in natural science from Oxford University, where he majored in physics and was the coxswain for a rowing team. At twenty-one years of age, having moved to Cambridge to take up research in the fields of general relativity and cosmology, he began to complain of feeling unusually clumsy. His mother persuaded him to visit a doctor. He was soon diagnosed as having a form of amyotrophic lateral sclerosis, commonly known in America as ALS, or Lou Gehrig's Disease. This disease attacks the motor neuron centers of the brain that control voluntary muscle activity, including the ability to walk (eventually, to move at all), to speak, to swallow, or even to breathe.

Hawking's condition overtook him so quickly that, at the time, he wasn't expected to live even long enough to complete his doctoral studies. Instead, he has survived 46 years from that time and become the most famous scientist living today. As Lucasian Professor of Mathematics at Cambridge University, he occupies the chair that once belonged to Sir Isaac Newton.

Over the years, Hawking's physical condition has atrophied to the point where he is completely paralyzed. He has not been able to feed himself for thirty-five years and has not been able to speak for nearly twenty-five years. Confined to a wheelchair, he can still move the muscles in his face a little; he communicates by using his cheek to type his thoughts into a computer program that then, through the mechanism of a voice synthesizer, speaks for him.

We look at Stephen Hawking, curled up in his wheelchair, unable to move or speak, and we see a man trapped in his own withered body, utterly helpless. At the same time, we see clearly that in that body resides a mind as strong as his body was when he was rowing at Oxford. We see a mind capable of traveling the lengths of the universe and grappling with the most complicated theories in abstract mathematics and physics.

Now, Hawking obviously believes that knowledge is possible. He assumes the essential reliability of his own thought processes as he ponders the physical universe and draws conclusions about its nature. If he didn't, he wouldn't bother to teach or write books about it.

The truth is, we *all* assume that true knowledge is possible. Those who say that "nothing can be known" and that "truth is relative" contradict themselves in the very act of proclaiming these things. If they really believed what they say, they wouldn't bother talking about it, and certainly not writing books about it. If nothing can be known and truth is relative, then who cares what each of us holds as true?

But, of course, the fact that those who assert this point of view continue to speak, teach, write, and attempt to influence others reveals their foundational belief in the reliability of human reasoning, the possibility of knowledge, and the existence of ultimate truth.

The theistic worldview can account for this and make sense of it. Just as with the issue of morality, so goes the issue of knowledge. Our belief in the reliability of human reasoning makes sense within the context of the Christian worldview. It fits.

After all, we do not see ourselves as "the wholly physical outcome of a purely physical process," to quote Paul Churchland once again.[57] We do not believe that we are the material products of an impersonal, unthinking material universe, but the special creation of the living God. God thinks; so do we. God reasons; so do we. Even as God is the source and standard of morality, so God is the source and standard of ideas, thought, and reason. We could even say that even as the laws of morality reflect the character of God, so the laws of logic reflect the thinking of God.

> Even as the laws of morality reflect the character of God, so the laws of logic reflect the thinking of God.

But Stephen Hawking does not believe in God. For him, the mind is a product of an unthinking *material* universe. How can that be?

We need to ask the atheist some questions about how he attempts to make his own lived experience of having a mind, and of knowing things, measure up to his materialistic worldview.

1. What is the mind?

Throughout history, human beings have described the mind as the intellectual capacity of the soul: the mind is the soul thinking. And, although we have always understood that the soul is in some mysterious manner related to the body, and the mind to the brain, we understood them to be distinct. The soul was not identical to the body; the mind was not identical to the brain. Rather, a human being was believed to be composed of a body *and* a soul.

This is essentially the Christian view of things. We demonstrate this common view even in the way we speak. Consider the teacher admonishing her student, "Emily, please, slow down and *use your brain.*" We've all heard and used such expressions.

But notice what's implied here. When our schoolteacher says, "Emily, please, slow down and use your brain," she assumes there is "someone" in Emily's body — a spirit, a soul — who is somehow distinct from her physical brain. And if Emily only tries, she *can* in fact use her brain to think. It's as though the teacher is saying, "Emily, God has given *you* a brain for you to use. So use *your* brain and work out the problem I've given you."

This kind of comment is not in the least strange to us because it's rooted in reality. You know, for example, that there is more to "you" than your body. You know instinctively that, in addition to your bodily members (eyes, legs, arms, ears, head, etc.), you also possess a whole range of purely immaterial things. You have "within you" memories, hopes, fears, goals, desires, emotions, beliefs, and the like. These things are just as much a part of "you" as your hands and feet. No one needs to tell you this. You *know* this instinctively and without a doubt.

God created each of us as a body-and-soul composite, and we know intuitively that our personal identity is better expressed by the word "soul" than by the word "brain."

> When it comes to the present scientific establishment, the *standard* belief is that the mind is no more than a product of brain chemistry.

Ask anyone who has watched someone die, perhaps a friend or a loved one. "One moment," he will tell you, "it was my *wife* lying there dying. The next moment, after she died, *she* was gone. Her spirit had left, and all that remained was her body. But that was not *her.*"

Atheists reject that kind of talk as mere "folk psychology." Atheists do not believe we are anything more than the bodies in which we dwell. They believe that we don't dwell *in* bodies at all — rather, that we *are* bodies and nothing more.

Atheists claim that there is no "you" apart from your body, and in particular your brain. You do not have a "mind" or "soul" or "spirit," because those are immaterial, spiritual, and therefore impossible, as the only things that exist are material.

2. If this is the case, what then are our thoughts and ideas?

Christians hold the commonsense view that our thoughts and ideas are the free activity of our minds.

But what would our thoughts and ideas be if naturalism were true? In his 1994 book *The Astonishing Hypothesis*, Francis Crick, one of the most well-known naturalist molecular biologists and neuroscientists, explained:

> The astonishing hypothesis is that "you," your joys and your sorrows, your memories and your ambitions, your sense of personal identity and free will, are in fact no more than the behavior of a vast assembly of nerve cells and their associated molecules ... The hypothesis is so alien to the ideas of most people alive today that it can truly be called astonishing.[58]

Of course, when Crick speaks of his hypothesis as being "alien to the ideas of most people alive today," he tacitly admits that ordinary men, women, and children know intuitively that there is more to the human person than "nerve cells and their associated molecules." Few people readily accept his view.

But when it comes to the present scientific establishment, the *standard* belief is that the mind is no more than a product of brain chemistry. "You, your joys and your sorrows, your memories and your ambitions, your sense of personal identity and free will, are in fact *no more than . . .*" material, chemical processes within your body. That and nothing more.

The philosopher Pierre Jean Georges Cabanis believed this. He stated his theory crudely but accurately, asserting that the human brain produces thoughts and ideas in much "the same way that the stomach and the bowels are destined to produce digestion" or "the liver to filter the bile."[59]

Charles Darwin's approach to naturalism, similarly, has yielded a widespread and deeply entrenched opinion among naturalists that such things as thoughts and beliefs are mere "excretions" of the brain.

3. But then, why in the world should we trust our thoughts to be true?

When a reductionist like Crick writes a book in order to explain that human thought is "nothing more than _____," he is forced to exempt *himself* from the reality he's describing. In effect he's saying, "All human thought is nothing more than the behavior of a vast assembly of nerve cells and their associated molecules, except for the thoughts I am expressing." If Crick really believed that his own ideas were included in the "no more than _____," he should instantly shove aside his keyboard and sally forth to do something more constructive than sitting at his desk with his brain excreting.

Philip Johnson comments:

> Imagine the reaction of the publisher if Crick had proposed to begin his book by announcing that "I, Francis Crick, my opinions and my science, and even the thoughts expressed in this book, consist of

nothing more than the behavior of a vast assembly
of nerve cells and their associated molecules." Few
browsers would be likely to read further.[60]

Atheists can *say* whatever they like about the nature of
the world we live in, but in the end they have to live in the
world God created. And lucky for those atheists who like
to think, and teach, and write books — in the world God
created, human minds are more than they imagine!

4. **If naturalism were true, and the "mind" is simply
    reducible to brain tissue and our thoughts, ideas,
    and knowledge are reducible to electrochemical
    processes within the brain, would not our thoughts
    and ideas in fact be *determined* by such processes?
    Wouldn't freedom of thought be an illusion?**

As freedom is a precondition of moral accountability,
so also is freedom a precondition of knowledge. How
could a man say he "knows" something to be "true" if
he is not free to think about options, form his own ideas,
deliberate, and choose what he accepts as true on the basis
of reason?

We wouldn't think to speak seriously of the
"knowledge" of a man forced at gunpoint to rattle off
what he had "learned" in a totalitarian government's
"reeducation" camp. A robot can be programmed to
verbalize arguments in favor of free trade, but no one
would speak of that robot as possessing "knowledge."
Likewise, would it be appropriate to speak of our
possessing "beliefs" and "knowledge" and "truth" if non-

rational physical processes in our brains have *determined* our ideas?

Here again, we find that common sense and the beliefs of ordinary people contradict what would be the case if naturalism were true. It certainly seems to us that our thoughts are free, doesn't it? We live our lives against the horizon of intentionality. Each of us goes through the day choosing to do some things and not others. We can make decisions, and reach conclusions every day, on a whole range of issues, because we are fundamentally free to do so.

We can also at any moment leap about the universe in our minds, thinking anything we like. We can think about a hamburger with mustard and pickles; about strange and as-yet undiscovered sea creatures swimming about at the bottom of the Mariana Trench; of the Trench itself as the subject for a new comic opera starring Felix the Cat and his "bag of tricks"; of lovely summer evenings, or the laws of logic, or a fine assortment of cosmetics. The silly and the sublime.

> We can at any moment leap about the universe in our minds, thinking anything we like.

We know, without anyone having to tell us, that our minds are free — and we continually operate on this basis. We assume freedom of mind and of thought in our educational, legal, and political institutions, in the arts, sciences, humanities, and religion — in every sphere of life. What possible meaning can concepts such as "knowledge" and "learning" have, though, if our "thoughts" are nothing more than physical processes occurring in our brains?

For example, why should we prosecute criminals? Mental activities such as thoughts, more often than not, precede the committing of crimes. But how could anyone ever be held responsible for the criminal consequences of his thoughts if his mind were not free?

Our belief in the essential freedom of the mind and of our thoughts makes sense the moment we embrace the truth of the Christian worldview. We believe that God creates us as body and soul and gives us minds that are free. So, it is reasonable for us to believe in the essential reliability of our thought processes. The existence of God, and our creation in the image of God, provide the metaphysical basis for our commonsense beliefs.

This is why we all (atheists included!) think like theists — and not as Francis Crick tells us we should. Even after writing his *Astonishing Hypothesis*, Crick probably continued to tell his students things like "Use your brains!"

You can see how the *reductio ad absurdum* demolishes the materialist worldview. It cannot stand logically because by its very nature it undercuts the *possibility* of any meaningful thought or exchange of thoughts whatsoever. If materialism were true, there would be no reason to debate the naturalist and Christian theistic worldviews: we'd be debating nothing more than a collection of brains excreting various chemicals in various quantities and combinations. You might as well argue over the fact that wind sometimes blows in one direction, sometimes in another; or that individual tongues of flame are variously higher or lower than other tongues of flame in a bonfire. So what if they are? It's all random, anyway. Who cares?

If atheists were truly consistent, they would have to shrug their shoulders and say nothing when a Christian declares his belief in God. In the final analysis, the Christian only thinks according to the physical processes operating in his brain, and the naturalist does the same. Neither of them can help it. So, as Phillip Johnson points out, academic naturalists like Arthur Kornberg should not be at all astonished "that otherwise intelligent and informed people, including physicians, are reluctant to believe that mind, as part of life, is matter and only matter." After all, writes Johnson:

> Presumably, one kind of chemical reaction in the brain causes Kornberg to accept materialist reductionism, while another kind of reaction cause those physicians to doubt it.[61]

If that is true, if that's how things really are, then why bother arguing about it? Some people simply *must* say, "Materialism is true," and others simply must say, "Materialism is not true." Their brain tissue and blind electrochemical processes occurring within that tissue randomly dictate what they call their "thoughts." And *that*, if naturalism *were true*, would be the end of the story — and not merely the story of this debate, but rather the story of all human thought.

5. **In a universe in which nothing exists but particular material substances, how does the naturalist account for the existence and authority of abstract entities such as the laws of logic — which are a part**

of what it means to reason rightly and come to true knowledge but are not material?

To come to knowledge of anything — algebra, geometry, chemistry, history, mechanics, finance — we must develop ideas in our minds. We must be able to reason about those ideas in a sound manner that will lead to valid conclusions.

Philosophers speak of the "laws of logic," the rules that distinguish good reasoning from bad reasoning. In his book *Socratic Logic*, Peter Kreeft explains what this means and why it's vitally important to our reply to the Godless delusion of atheism:

> Logic has power: the power of proof and thus persuasion. Any power can be rightly used or abused. The power of logic is rightly used to win the truth and defeat error; it is wrongly used to win the *argument* and defeat your opponent. Argument is to truth as fishing is to fish, or war to peace, or courtship to marriage. The power of logic comes from the fact that it is the science and art of argument. . . . Whether you use logic for right or wrong ends, it is a powerful tool. No matter what your thought's end or goal or purpose may be, it will attain that end more effectively if it is clearer and more logical.[62]

To take a classic example of a logical syllogism: "If all men are mortal, and Socrates is a man, then it follows with certainty that Socrates is mortal." This is an example of sound reasoning. Of course, if one or both of the premises in the syllogism were false — let's say that not all men are mortal, or that Socrates is not a man — then the conclusion that Socrates is mortal would not logically follow. But given the truth of the premises, the conclusion not only follows; it follows *inescapably*.

An example of bad or erroneous reasoning would be for one to argue that Socrates is mortal because "my mother says so," or that Socrates is mortal because "you're an idiot," or that Socrates is *not* mortal because "the man who taught me he was mortal turned out to be a communist," or Socrates is mortal because "all normal, thinking people know he was mortal."

Logicians have technical names for each of these logical fallacies,[63] as well as for the rules of good and sound reasoning, but the point here is simply that the act of reasoning, and reasoning "rightly," is absolutely necessary to gain knowledge and come to truth.

In this book, when we speak of the laws of logic,[64] or even of ideas, we are speaking of entities that are *non-material*. You will never discover an idea that is four feet in length, or a law of logic that weighs six ounces, or a logical fallacy abandoned along the roadside or forming on the surface of a stagnant pond.

> You will never discover an idea that is four feet in length, or a law of logic that weighs six ounces, or a logical fallacy abandoned along the roadside or forming on the surface of a stagnant pond.

Material things are by nature concrete. They have parts and take up space. They are particular and changing. Ideas, on the other hand, are purely immaterial; they are abstract, do not take up space, and are universal and unchanging. This description of ideas holds true, always and everywhere, with the laws of logic.

Let's test this principle on something as common as the concept of an equilateral triangle.

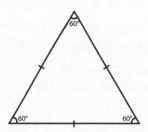

The idea you have of that triangle right now in your mind's eye is purely abstract. It is not made of any material substance, it is not concrete, not made of atoms, takes up no space, and is not susceptible to change.

The triangle concept you hold in your mind is universal in that it applies to all equilateral triangles anywhere in the universe and is not merely the concept of a *particular* triangle. But notice something very intriguing: This concept of the triangle that you see in your mind's eye, so to speak, *is located in a particular place*. It really exists as a concept *inside your mind*. Remember, this idea takes up no space, but it is really there. You know that it is, because you have the idea of this triangle clearly in mind right now.

Notice also that this idea you have is unchanging. In order for a triangle to *be* a triangle, it must have three sides. Anything else is not a triangle.

Now, imagine a particular triangle: the iron triangle that hangs on the porch of Grandma's house. When it's dinnertime, Grandma calls everyone in by ringing that triangle nice and loud. That triangle is material (i.e., made of iron); it is particular (i.e., it exists in one particular place — Grandma's porch — as a concrete reality, not an immaterial concept); and it is changeable (i.e., in time, it will weather, rust, and eventually disintegrate).

But — unlike Grandma's dinner-bell triangle — ideas, concepts, mathematics, and the laws of logic are all *immaterial*. So, what happens when an atheist who insists that *the only things that exist are natural, material objects* tries to account for the existence of immaterial things, like knowledge, ideas, and concepts, which are by nature abstract, universal, and unchanging?

Let's see.

First, if he says that immaterial things like the "laws of logic" exist, he proves his own worldview to be false, because he's already said that "all is matter." But if he says the laws of logic don't exist, then how does he explain their authority in the realm of thought and knowledge?

And make no mistake, the atheist-naturalist takes pride in asserting that the laws of logic are authoritative and should be obeyed, whatever else he may say about immaterial things. If he employs the rules of logic to demonstrate beyond question that all men are mortal, and that Socrates is a man, he *expects* you to accept the conclusion that Socrates is mortal.

It will not go well with you if you retort:

> Oh, well, I admit that the "laws of logic" dictate the conclusion, but I don't accept the existence or authority of the laws of logic. Instead, I believe

whatever my hairdresser tells me, and she tells me that Socrates was definitely immortal.

A person voicing such sentiment would be immediately recognized as either insane, a joker, or just plain stupid.

Second, if the atheist denies that immaterial things such as knowledge and logic actually exist, apart from the electro-chemical "excretions" taking place in the brain that, he claims, account for them, then he is being consistent in one sense and inconsistent in another. He's consistent by adhering to his strict materialist worldview, however absurd the conclusions of this argument are. But he is being inconsistent by asking you to *accept* and *agree with* his position. For if his theory is — as he claims — merely the material residue of his cerebral functions, then how can that *transfer* to your brain? How does his matter-based "idea" move through time and space from inside his head to inside yours? Be aware that any appeals to fall-back arguments — like linguistics, symbols, gestures, and facial expressions that "convey meaning" — beg the question and do not in the slightest resolve his dilemma.

THE PROBLEM OF "OUGHTNESS"

All of us, atheists included, instinctively perceive that the purpose of human reason is to arrive at the truth. We all reason our way toward true conclusions in things large and small — whether it's balancing the checkbook, telling the time of day, or deciding whether it's harmful to your health to wolf down a second heaping helping of cheese fries.

> Everyone understands that he ought to embrace the truth when he discovers it.

Everyone understands that he ought to embrace the truth when he discovers it. For example, you *ought* to accept the demonstrable fact that 2 + 2 = 4; you *ought* to agree that if all As are Green and all Bs are Yellow then no As can be Bs, etc. And this is just as true with regard to moral laws — which, like the laws of logic, don't describe *what* people do but, rather, what people *ought* to do. Just as there is an "oughtness" to the laws of logic, there is an "oughtness" to moral laws, too. These, also, don't describe how people act but, rather, how people *ought* to act. Even atheists will say that you *shouldn't* (ought not to) kill someone; you shouldn't steal; and you shouldn't kick a blind beggar sitting on the sidewalk. Atheists appeal to certain, well defined, universally recognized and — most important for our discussion here — *immaterial* laws that prescribe how people should act.

If premise A is true (all men are mortal) and premise B is also true (Socrates is a man), then everyone "ought" to acquiesce to the conclusion that rationally follows (Socrates is mortal). Atheists as well as Christians believe this. And in each case, it is a belief in things — laws — that are *immaterial*.

But here's the problem: If materialism is true . . . and if the idea you have in your mind that that all men are mortal is simply a particular "brain state" brought about by certain electrochemical reactions in your head . . . and if the idea you have in your mind that Socrates is a man is simply another brain state, brought about by another electrochemical reaction in your head . . . then it is quite difficult to understand how this *ought* to lead to a third brain state of believing that Socrates is mortal. Think about that.

How can we say that one *ought* to accept a "rational necessity" and to accept the "logical conclusion" of an "abstract argument" about whether Socrates is mortal or not, when, as atheists tell us, our very thoughts and ideas are material functions of the brain that are blindly determined by "physical necessity"?

Of course, none of this is a problem for the Christian, because theism is not a reductionist worldview. It *includes* not only the impersonal, material world but also non-material beings such as God, angels, and human souls; non-natural properties such as moral laws; and abstract entities such as the laws of logic and mathematics. The Christian worldview is broad enough to account for the richness of real experience.

Because God exists, the preconditions exist for both moral law and laws of reason. And because God has created human beings in His image, as living and free souls, the preconditions exist for moral accountability and rational thought, knowledge, and truth.

This is why we can think, reason, and read. Christianity can easily account for this harmony. Atheism cannot.

THE ELIMINATION OF NATURALISM

So how do atheists deal with these questions and challenges? It's a difficult problem for them. While so many aspects of human experience don't seem to be reducible to matter, the atheist cannot allow anything to exist that doesn't fit the Procrustean bed of naturalism. Every aspect of our rich human experience must be explainable — or be *made* "explainable" in the violent fashion of old Procrustes — for atheists to avoid the logical pitfalls all around them.

Naturalists cannot admit anything that might be irreducibly mental, abstract, or immaterial — which is to say, *spiritual*. While an atheist can accept the notion of matter that thinks, he cannot allow the slimmest possibility that the mind might in some sense be *distinct* from matter. This opens the door to the possibility of non-natural explanations, such as the existence of God and the human soul, which he simply cannot tolerate.

Naturalism as a philosophical system hasn't been *demonstrated* to be true; it's *assumed* to be true. But this means that the naturalist *must* in some way explain everything in human experience as being reducible to matter. If this requires that human experience be stretched out of recognition or trimmed down to make it "fit," so be it. Whatever he can't explain according to atheism's rigid orthodoxy, he must conclude does not exist, and therefore dismiss as a mere "illusion."

This is the heart of the Godless delusion.

> Naturalists cannot admit anything that might be irreducibly mental, abstract, or immaterial — which is to say, *spiritual*.

Paul Churchland is known for his teaching of "eliminative materialism," also referred to as "physicalism."[65] Churchland seeks to apply a consistent materialism to the issue of the human mind. He first solves the problem of how to explain the existence of non-material entities in a materialist universe by denying their existence. He simply eliminates them.

Churchland writes:

> The important point about the standard evolutionary story is that the human species and all of its features are the wholly physical outcome of a purely physical process. If this is the correct account of our origin, then there seems neither need nor room to fit any nonphysical substances or properties into our theoretical accounts of ourselves. We are creatures of matter.[66]

Churchland believes that the commonsense understanding of the mind that most human beings have always had is mistaken. He refers to this common understanding as "folk psychology." He thinks that as scientists come to an ever more complete understanding of the brain, many of the mental states for which we have traditionally used words like "desire," "intend," "believe," "love," and even "pain," will be seen not to exist at all. He speculates that even consciousness may not actually exist but be something of an illusion. What will be seen to exist are brains, nerves, particular electrochemical reactions, the firing of neurons, central nervous system activities, and so forth.

Procrustes was kinder to his victims than the materialist: he only lopped off the feet of his guests, while the materialist lops off our heads to make us fit the iron bed of his worldview! But when the materialist eliminates a mind that is free in favor of one whose very ideas are determined by physical processes, he eliminates the validity of his own thoughts. His worldview is self-refuting.

NON-ANSWERS TO QUESTIONS ABOUT THE MIND

While some atheists attempt to deal with the problems raised about naturalism's understanding of the mind, many don't bother with them at all. Those who do deal with them tend to do so only superficially and, therefore, wholly inadequately.

For instance, John Searle attributes our ability to think, reason, and read to an accident of evolution. He claims that human beings evolved a "surplus of neurons" and, therefore, mental abilities far above and beyond what we really needed to hunt, gather, survive, and reproduce. While he admits that recognizing ourselves to be essentially baboons with a surplus of neurons could cast doubt on the reliability of our thinking, he says that all we can do is trust our minds, at least provisionally, so that we can go on doing science and so test the limits of our mental abilities by the results we get.[67]

This is what we might refer to as the "well, our minds seem to be working okay" answer to the question of why we should trust the thoughts determined by electrochemical processes in the brain. But this is no answer at all. The fact that the naturalist's thoughts "work" says nothing for the naturalist case. Maybe his thoughts work precisely because *naturalism* isn't true, and our minds are what the Christians have always said they are.

> The naturalist worldview cannot account for the reliability of the human mind — and, therefore, cannot account for the successes of science.

Sometimes, an atheist points to successes of science as a way of answering the questions the Christian raises about the reliability of the mind. The argument goes something like this:

> You try to make it seem that we have no reason to trust our thinking. But notice that there are millions of naturalists who think rationally and have made progress in every field of science. We've sent men to the moon! Don't the results we've achieved in the fields of mathematics and medicine and engineering and biochemistry and every other field of knowledge demonstrate the essential reliability of our minds?

If Christian arguments challenging atheism entailed the notion that naturalists don't use reason and don't come to true conclusions about anything, then maybe this rebuttal would have some weight. But these are not our arguments. We contend that the naturalist worldview cannot account for the reliability of the human mind — and, therefore, cannot account for the successes of science. If our thoughts are mere "excretions of brain," *then* we have no reason to trust them, and knowledge is impossible.

As British evolutionary biologist J. B. S. Haldane wrote:

> If my mental processes are determined wholly by the motions of atoms in my brain, I have no reason to suppose that my beliefs are true . . . and hence I have no reason for supposing my brain to be composed of atoms.[68]

The fact that naturalistic scientists *do* think and reason, and *are* successful, is evidence that their mental processes are *not* determined wholly by the motions of atoms in their brains. Their thought processes work because their minds are what the Christian, not the naturalist, says they are.

In the end, the only case that a naturalist can make for the reliability of the human mind is the argument of evolution: that random mutations brought about the human ability to reason, that natural selection then rewarded creatures that could think and draw correct conclusions, and that — in essence — our minds evolved reliability through trial and error.

This is the path that Stephen Hawking takes:

> Provided the universe has evolved in a regular way, we might expect that the reasoning abilities that natural selection has given us would be valid ... and so would not lead us to the wrong conclusions.[69]

On purely on materialist grounds, this argument is entirely circular. In a universe in which nothing exists but matter, our minds would be reducible to brain chemistry. Our thoughts, ideas, and even our reasoning would be reducible to deterministic physical processes like the processes by which the liver filters bile or the stomach digests. So when Hawking appeals to the theory of evolution, random mutation, and natural selection to explain our ability to *think, reason, and draw accurate conclusions*, he appeals to a theory that is itself *the result of physical processes*. Then how can Hawking possibly know that his ideas on random mutation and natural selection are true?

Phillip Johnson appropriately describes this argument as a "hall of mirrors with no exit." In his book *Reason in the Balance*, he writes:

> A theory that is the product of a mind can never adequately explain the mind that produced the theory. The story of the great scientific mind that discovers absolute truth is satisfying only so long as we accept the mind itself as a given. Once we try to explain the mind as a product of its own discoveries, we are in a hall of mirrors with no exit.[70]

If the mind is seen as independent of the world of strict material cause and effect, then we can celebrate the stories of the great scientific minds that discover amazing things — stories like that of Copernicus, Newton, Einstein, and even Stephen Hawking. But if it turns out that their brilliant ideas are nothing but the biological product of deterministic material laws and natural processes, biochemical excretions, and whatnot, what's there to admire?

It's a bit like reading a naturalist version of *Sleeping Beauty* and learning that love's first kiss does not come from the handsome prince, but rather from an electro-chemical kissing machine.

The story loses its magic, don't you think?

THE GODLESS CONTRADICTION

An atheist exists in a state of tension brought about by the contradiction between what he says is true about the world and what he, as a human being, knows to be true. The atheist *knows* that knowledge is possible. He claims to champion human reason and knowledge, assumes the reliability of human reason every day of his life, and desires to be rational. But he holds to a worldview that is *constantly forcing him in the direction of irrationality.* It reduces his mind to brain chemistry and his beliefs, knowledge, and truth to brain states that may turn out to be illusions. He wants to use the laws of logic and seek knowledge and truth, and he believes that all this is possible, yet he holds a view of the world that cannot even account for the existence of reason or the laws of logic, much less their reliability.

The evidence that his worldview must be wrong is everywhere about him and within him — in his desire for knowledge; in his ability to think, reason, and draw right conclusions; in every idea he ponders and every sentence he speaks; even in his ability to read the words on this page.

So what are the atheist's options?

One, he can admit that the naturalist worldview destroys the very possibility of knowledge, eliminates it, is a *reductio ad absurdum,* and, therefore, cannot be true.

Two, he can turn from naturalism and contemplate the fact that God's existence alone can make sense of his experience in this area of knowledge.

Or, three, he can suppress the evidence, give up on rationalism, put his fingers in his ears, and chant, "La, la, la, la, la, la, I can't hear you!" in his attempt to avoid the possibility that God exists.

Atheists often say, "We must be rational, and that is why I cannot believe all this superstitious Christian nonsense about 'God.' We must have a rational foundation for our knowledge that is scientific and based on the laws of logic and evidences." But as soon as you show him that without God he has no basis for trusting his thoughts or believing in the laws of logic, he will switch and say, "But of course, ultimately, this is a chance universe and no one can know anything for sure."

Here's how one Protestant author describes the atheist's situation:

> The unbeliever wants to be rational, but holds an irrational view of the universe. He denies the possibility of true knowledge even while he pursues knowledge and tells us we don't know what we're talking about. He says in essence, "Nobody knows for sure, but I'm sure you're wrong!" The unbeliever wants to be rational enough to say we are wrong and irrational enough to say, "I don't have to give you a foundation for my knowledge."[71]

In other words, the atheist says, "I know that you believers in God are wrong. The fact that I can't explain to you how thinking might arise naturally from non-thinking material substances doesn't matter. I still know that you're wrong."

Ultimately, naturalism reduces to utter skepticism. If the atheist were consistent with what he says is true about the nature of the world, he would abandon reason. But of course, he can't, because for him to give up reason would be "reasonable" in his situation, and therefore inconsistent with his worldview. Atheism destroys the possibility of knowledge. If atheism were true, we could know nothing at all, including the "fact" that atheism was true.

On the other hand, when it comes to this issue of worldviews and knowledge, the proof that God exists is that the foundation of any "proof" at all requires God's existence. If God does not exist, the reliability of the reasoning process is undermined: ideas, thinking, and reasoning are mere chemical reactions, and "knowledge" and "truth" are meaningless terms. But the very notion of "proof" is rooted in the validity of the reasoning process — and this only makes sense in a universe in which God exists.

And so, as one Protestant philosopher was fond of saying, "The proof of God's existence is that without him you can't prove anything." The very notion of "proof" presupposes the existence of God.

Even to argue against God's existence, the atheist must first presuppose it. The atheist wants to use ideas, reasoning, and logic to argue against God's existence, yet holds to a worldview that cannot account for ideas, reasoning, and logic. If he wants to use ideas, reason, and logic to argue against God's existence, he must first borrow those weapons from the theistic worldview that makes sense of them and can account for them. These weapons simply cannot be forged in the reductionist factory of naturalist atheism. So, in other words, he must first *accept* God's existence — then, if he likes, he can try to disprove it.

The final irony is that when an atheist chooses knowledge, reason, and logic as his weapons of war against God, ultimately they backfire on him.

CHAPTER SEVEN

THE "DO AS I SAY, NOT AS I DO" HYPOCRISY OF ATHEISM

As Darwin clearly recognized, we are not entitled — not on evolutionary grounds, at any rate — to regard our own adaptive behavior as "better" or "higher" than that of a cockroach, who, after all, is adapted equally well to life in its own environmental niche.

— James Rachels

People everywhere intuitively know that human life is precious and should be protected. Those who act against this intuition are known as sociopaths. When sociopaths like Hitler, Stalin, and Mao gain power, society quickly descends into chaos, violence, and oppression. William Golding's searing novel *Lord of the Flies* vividly depicts the inevitable human propensity toward degeneration and violence once the restraining forces of virtue and "common decency" have been removed.

Atheism enables sociopathic behavior by claiming that human life has no intrinsic, transcendent value. That's why, as atheism gains ascendency in the West, there is a concomitant rise in barbaric, inhumane practices such as abortion, fetal stem cell research, cloning, infanticide,[72] and euthanasia.[73] Society's death spiral into darkness, despair, and nihilism is being propelled by naturalism. With Nietzsche's proclamation that "God is dead" came the death knell of modern man's acknowledgment of, and respect for, objective truth, transcendent values, natural law, and a God-given code of morality.

Unfounded Values

Atheists claim to possess truth and values, and many live what could be called "good" lives of service to others and obedience to secular law — what we might think of as "niceness" — but in the end, they cannot escape the *reductio ad absurdum* in which they are prisoners.[74]

W. T. Jones, in his *History of Western Philosophy*, elaborates on the implication for values of a worldview that believes the "real" to consist only of that which science can demonstrate:

> Think, for instance, of the role instruments play in the accession of factual knowledge. Where would physics be without precise measurement? Astronomy without the telescope? Biology without the microscope? But these instruments, which have helped us discover innumerable physical, astronomical, and biological facts, throw no light at all on values. When we dissect a body in the laboratory we do not find the courage or magnanimity the owner of that body exemplified. Nor do our microscopes or telescopes show us God or freedom or immortality. So far as we believe that these instruments, and the techniques they imply, give us the whole truth about the universe, it is clear that God, freedom, and immortality, courage, justice and piety are not objective realities at all.[75]

This perfectly describes the Godless delusion. Except for sociopaths, atheists cannot bring themselves to actually *live* according to the above claim that good and bad, immorality and morality, are not objective realities.

Why? Because to embrace such lunacy would mean there is no objective difference in helping an old lady across the street versus whacking her on the head with a baseball bat and stealing her purse. And yet, atheists know there *is* a clear, objective difference between extending a helping hand and wielding a baseball bat.

British philosopher Dr. Michael Ruse admits with brutal consistency that, on the basis of his evolutionary naturalist worldview, the notion of "ethics" is purely illusory.

> Considered as a rationally justifiable set of claims about an objective something, [ethics] is illusory. I appreciate that when somebody says "Love thy neighbor as thyself," they think they are referring above and beyond themselves. Nevertheless, such reference is truly without foundation. . . . Morality is just an aid to survival and reproduction. . . . Morality is an ephemeral product of the evolutionary process. . . . It has no existence or being beyond this and any deeper meaning is illusory.[76]

One can only wonder if Dr. Ruse actually would be willing to live his life according to his "ethics are not real but only illusory" theory. What would he do, for example, upon discovering that a plagiarist had filched from his many books and written a plagiarized "best seller"

> When it's *their* money or *their* lives being threatened, atheists quickly appeal to ethical standards that are suddenly far from "illusory."

that was a rip-off of Ruse's own work? Our guess is that Dr. Ruse would pick up his phone, call his lawyer, and initiate a lawsuit against the plagiarist.

He would be right to do all this, because what the plagiarist did was *wrong* — not because Dr. Ruse's own personal, illusory system of morality said so, but because the action in itself *was* wrong. We have no doubt that any atheist would stand up for his rights if they were being infringed upon illegally. When it's *their* money or *their* lives being threatened, atheists quickly appeal to ethical standards that are suddenly far from "illusory."

HUMAN WORTH AND DIGNITY: SAY ONE THING, DO ANOTHER

In July 2002, an explosion in a Pennsylvania coal mine left nine men trapped 240 feet underground in a dark, frigid, partially flooded mineshaft. Rescue teams immediately snapped into action. No expense was spared in the effort to locate and extract the men from their subterranean nightmare.

For three days, Americans were transfixed by the dramatic rescue effort, many praying the miners would survive. Happily, they were rescued. Millions of people heaved a collective sigh of relief, though none of them had ever met or even previously heard of the nine men.

That disaster-with-a-happy-ending reveals an undeniable truth about who and what human beings are: They are precious, with an objective value and dignity that utterly transcends what they do for a living, how much money they have, or how physically attractive they may be.

Everyone, including atheists, knows this truth. Atheists *act* as if it is true, even as they vehemently deny it. (*"What* value?" one can almost hear Hitler, Stalin, Mao, and the rest of the twentieth century's atheist mass-murderers muttering to themselves.)

Only the existence of God can make sense of, and fully account for, this universal human intuition regarding the objective value of human beings. Atheism cannot.

This is why, when challenging the Godless delusion, it is important to point out its inherent hypocrisy. "Do as I say, not as I do" summarizes the unbridgeable chasm between the naturalist's professed worldview and the *real-world* attitude with which they live their lives.

Because atheism holds that human beings are just accidents of nature, purely physical, and devoid of a "soul," the practical outcome of the atheism theory is to treat human beings as hardly more than "living machines." These are subjectively valuable only insofar as they produce, entertain, provide pleasure, or in some other way provide a benefit to another. The ubiquity of pornography has fueled this dehumanizing mindset.

Most atheists have likely never thought this issue through. And most would probably respond with raised eyebrows and expressions of incredulity if a Christian were to tell him that if the atheist worldview were true, there would be no basis for believing in human value and dignity. Some atheists, however, have thought through the implications of their position and freely admit them.

According to the evolutionist George Gaylord Simpson, the meaning of evolution is that "man is the result of a purposeless and natural process that did not have him in mind. He was not planned."[77]

Another example of this bleak view of human beings as meaningless is found in a biology textbook used for years in many American high schools:

> Some shrink from the conclusion that the human species was not designed, has no purpose, and is the product of mere mechanical mechanisms — but this seems to be the message of evolution.[78]

Human beings are nothing more than the purposeless products of mechanical mechanisms? Sadly, that's what many educators are teaching our children, high schoolers, and college students in classrooms across the land. But no one ever asks those educators why anyone should care when nine "purposeless products of mechanical mechanisms" become trapped in a flooded mineshaft.

Since human persons quite obviously have inequalities of "merit" — inequalities of gifting, talent, ability, personality, character, contribution to society, etc. — why is it that we seem to have this universal intuition and strong belief that each human being possesses equal value and should be treated with equal dignity?

Political philosopher Joel Feinberg pondered this exact question. His conclusion was that this intuition and belief, however universal, has no grounding whatsoever in the natural world and seems to be some kind of irrational and unjustifiable attitude we have. It's just a subjective feeling that we are worth something. We, in fact, are not.[79]

If that were true, however, then how could one speak of human beings as possessing intrinsic and equal dignity, the pricelessness with which all intuitively understand human persons to have? Even Charles Darwin chafed at this "intolerable" cognitive dissonance between naturalism and his own innate recognition that human beings have an objective value:

> [T]he view held by most physicists, namely that the sun with all the planets will in time grow too cold for life . . . Believing as I do that man in the distant future will be a far more perfect creature than he now is, *it is an intolerable thought that he and all other sentient beings are doomed to complete annihilation* after such long-continued slow progress.[80]

Moreland comments brilliantly on Darwin's words:

> It is just not clear how, on a naturalist view, humans have any intrinsic value at all. . . . If Darwin's point above is correct, then we current humans have less value than future humans and, in fact, may be properly treated as means to the end of evolving greater creatures. We stand to future products of evolution as amoebas stand to us. . . . [H]umans are just one fleeting stage in evolutionary development that is moving towards higher and higher life forms. All intermediate stages from amoebas to humans have only instrumental value as they contribute to later stages. Earlier stages do not have intrinsic value. In fact [some naturalist scientists have stated] it is only the DNA program in humans that has intrinsic value, and we exist to perfect that program to bring about future life.[81]

So is there any escape from the iron logic of naturalism — that human beings have no intrinsic, transcendent value and dignity?

American atheist philosopher James Rachels says no.

> They have not survived the colossal shift of perspective brought about by Darwin's theory. It might be thought that this result need not be devastating for the idea of human dignity, because even if the traditional supports are gone, the idea might still be defended on some other grounds. Once again, though, an evolutionary perspective is bound to make one skeptical. The doctrine of human dignity says that humans merit a level of moral concern wholly different from that accorded to mere animals; for this to be true, there would have to be some big, morally significant difference between them. Therefore, any adequate defense of human dignity would require some conception of human beings as radically different from other animals. But that is precisely what evolutionary theory calls into question. It makes us suspicious of any doctrine that sees large gaps of any sort between humans and all other creatures. This being so, a Darwinian may conclude that a successful defense of human dignity is most unlikely.[82]

This is the ugly-faced reality of atheism.

Indeed, some naturalists within the radical environmentalist movement do not shy away from insisting, for instance, that a human being is worth no more than a chicken. The president of PETA (People for the Ethical Treatment of Animals), Ingrid Newkirk, declared:

Animal liberationists do not separate out the human animal, so there is no rational basis for saying that a human being has special rights. *A rat is a pig is a dog is a boy. They are all mammals.*[83]

This same woman also offered a chilling assessment of the "intrinsic value" of human beings:

Humans have grown like a cancer. We're the biggest blight on the face of the earth.[84]

In the wake of the recent devastating 2010 Haitian earthquake, however — curiously enough — we didn't see news stories of atheists being willing to publicly say that the poor suffering Haitians had no more intrinsic value than chickens, and that there was no objective reason why they should be shown any more concern than that shown to chickens. Don't hold your breath waiting for *that* to happen, because fortunately, atheists don't practice what they preach. Just thank God that once again, while the naturalist is willing to talk the logical implications of his worldview, he is rarely willing to live them.

For example, Richard Dawkins describes the world as one with "at bottom, no design, no purpose, no evil and no good, nothing but blind, pitiless indifference."[85] But if Dawkins' claim is true, then how would an atheist account for his belief that his own daughter is worth more than a rat? Yes, he is emotionally attached to her, but why should he have a problem if a human trafficker were to abduct and sell the girl into a life of forced prostitution? If what Dawkins says is true, then wouldn't the human trafficker who abducts and sells someone's daughter into the sex trade really just being consistent with atheist principles?

To the atheist who says, "No!" we say, "Why not?"

Whenever opportunities arise, Christians should *challenge* atheists to defend their faith in a purely material universe by exposing the *reductio ad absurdum* of their worldview. We should show them that they cannot make sense of what they know in their hearts to be true about human dignity.

OF PERSONS AND COCKROACHES

Some atheists will attempt to defend their belief in human value and dignity on the basis of "personhood." They say that since each person has a life, friends, family, likes and dislikes, desires, and abilities; and since each person makes choices, creates, loves and is loved, and contributes in some way to society, these subjective qualities serve as sufficient grounds in themselves for believing that human beings have value.

The problem with such an attempt to reconcile naturalism with human value and dignity is clear. From a strictly evolutionary point of view, such a rationale smacks of "speciesism"— which folks such as Ingrid Newkirk define as prejudice and discrimination based upon species. Or, as James Rachels put it:

> As Darwin clearly recognized, we are not entitled — not on evolutionary grounds, at any rate — to regard our own adaptive behavior as 'better' or 'higher' than that of a cockroach, who, after all, is adapted equally well to life in its own environmental niche.[86]

Naturalists do not consider our ability as human beings to love and be loved, dream, plan, create, or contribute to society, as legitimate justification for viewing people as more valuable than cockroaches. The Christian worldview holds that distinction; according to the atheist worldview, it would be impossible.[87]

> Naturalists do not consider our ability as human beings to love and be loved, dream, plan, create, or contribute to society, as legitimate justification for viewing people as more valuable than cockroaches.

Think about it. If atheism *were* true, Ingrid Newkirk's repulsive comments would merely express the brutal, naked fact of the matter. Human beings could not claim any intrinsic value above that of a sheep, a rat, or a paramecium. Of course, if atheism is correct, we could all pretend that we do — just as the atheist who believes his daughter is more valuable than a rat would be pretending as well.

But who would want to live in that universe? Who *could* live in that universe? No one would, not even atheists. Which is why, no matter what absurd things they say, they are not willing to *live* according to those absurdities. They are forced to live the double life that their Godless delusion ruthlessly imposes on them; one half in the fantasy world of atheism, the world in which all that exists is matter, the other half in the real world.

No wonder there is so much nihilism, so much despair and "lostness" among young people these days.[88] We wonder why the music of recent decades is so filled with expressions of rage, fear, antisocial rants, and outright violence. Compare it to the popular music written in earlier generations, even during times of war, such as the Civil

War or World War II. That music is dramatically happier and more hopeful than much of what is popular today.

No wonder so many young people these days are so mixed up. Modern parents try to help their children have higher self-esteem and a stronger sense of worth as persons. But our culture teaches them to believe that they are meaningless accidents of a material evolution. To quote their high school biology teacher, they have "no ultimate purpose," and are really just "the product of mere mechanical mechanisms."

Even if just subconsciously, our children perceive and act upon the implications of the atheist-naturalist worldview being force-fed to them across practically all avenues of modern media. As they begin to process the meaning of what they're being told — that they're not created by God, and they have no ultimate purpose — even if they never understand the dismal ramifications of naturalism, they surely feel its deleterious effects, morally, emotionally, spiritually, psychologically, and socially. If you doubt this, turn on MTV and observe for yourself the dire effects on our culture that have resulted from decades of atheist propagandizing.

Better yet . . . don't.

HUMAN RIGHTS

Modern Americans — like most Westerners living in developed countries — are big talkers when it comes to human rights. These two words have become a meaningless slogan that resonates well with the average man and woman. It flows effortlessly from the chattering mouths of inane celebrities, obsequious politicians, and vacuous television news anchors. "Human rights!" they all cry. But what exactly does that mean?

According to Washington, Jefferson, Adams, and the other principal Founding Fathers, it had something to do with "life, liberty, and the pursuit of happiness" which, they affirmed all human beings "are endowed by their Creator with." They spoke of these as "certain unalienable rights."

THE RIGHT TO LIFE

The inalienable right to life of every innocent human individual is a *constitutive element of a civil society and its legislation.*

The inalienable rights of the person must be recognized and respected by civil society and the political authority. These human rights depend neither on single individuals nor on parents; nor do they represent a concession made by society and the state; they belong to human nature and are inherent in the person by virtue of the creative act from which the person took his origin. Among such fundamental rights one should mention in this regard every human being's right to life and physical integrity from the moment of conception until death.

— *Catechism of the Catholic Church* 2273

Jesus Christ declared that the fundamental human right of all people is to be truly free to know and love God, who created them:

> "You will know the truth, and the truth will make you free."
>
> — Jn 8:32

Atheism, on the other hand, can speak of human rights in only the narrowest of senses. Would human beings really possess rights in a naturalist universe? If so, on what basis would they have them? Where would such "rights" come from? On purely scientific grounds, how would a material cosmos have the capacity to endow randomly generated things with "rights"? What "rights" would rocks have? What "rights" would light waves have? On what basis would human beings, say, be entitled to more "rights" than cockroaches?

If God does *not* exist and there is nothing beyond the material universe, how could "rights" arise naturally from endless chemical interactions or from physical particles randomly jostling one another?

So, if it isn't the material universe that bestows human rights, then who or what does? Is it our family or tribe? Does the society in which we live endow us with human rights? Does the State? Or does the individual man or woman establish his own set of "human rights" to which he lays claim by sheer force of his or her own will?

The problem with any of these possibilities, of course, is that any right granted by some person or group of persons is a right that can easily be taken away at the whim of the grantor.

> How could "rights" arise naturally from endless chemical interactions or from physical particles randomly jostling one another?

Historically, kings could raise a man to riches and glory or send him off to be burned alive — in an instant, with the mere lifting of a finger. In officially atheist regimes, such as China, North Korea, and the former Soviet Union, it is the State that grants "rights" to the individual — and the State can remove any or all of them at will. The late famous Russian dissident, Aleksandr Solzhenitsyn, terrifyingly describes his firsthand experience with the atheistic Soviet model of "human rights" in his landmark book *The Gulag Archipelago*. In secular democracies, the "people" ostensibly grant themselves and their governmental agents rights — and the people can take them away via the ballot box.

When we speak of "human rights," we typically have in mind either those "rights" that are granted by a secular authority which can, rightfully, legally, revoke them — in the U.S., the right to vote is revoked in the case of convicted criminals — or rights that are intrinsic and, as the Founding Fathers described them, *inalienable*. These rights, such as the right to life, men and women possess by virtue of their nature as human beings.

These are Rights with a capital R. They are God-given, true, and valid, and they exist, regardless of whatever anyone may say and whether or not the state acknowledges them. These are rights no power on earth can rightfully take away because no power on earth can grant them. Only God can.

As the Declaration of Independence states:

> We hold these truths to be self-evident, that all men are created equal, that they are endowed by their Creator with certain unalienable Rights, that among these are Life, Liberty and the pursuit of Happiness . . .

Only our Creator can endow us with rights that are unalienable — rights that cannot be taken away by any human power. Our Founding Fathers understood this truth. In a godless universe comprised of nothing but material substances, time, and chance, there is no one to bestow these kinds of rights.

However, the Christian theistic worldview can account for both the existence of unalienable human rights and our intuitive recognition of, and yearning for, such rights. If God exists, then intrinsic and unalienable human rights exist. But the only "rights" someone living in a truly atheist universe could possibly possess would be those he wrested for himself through violence. In fact, atheism's situational ethics and moral relativism is a sure-fire prescription for wiping out a society — indeed, a civilization — once the protective seawall of traditional, theistic morality is breached and the churning tsunami of human pathologies such as greed, lust, violence, and racism come rushing in.

When the atheist worldview claws its way to ascendancy in a given culture, sweeping away all restraints of religion, morality, and human rights, we see the rise of murderous totalitarian regimes.

Hitler. Stalin. Mao. Pol Pot. Don't forget them. They are the ultimate face of atheism. They represent the logical conclusion of atheism's denial that nothing objective, transcendent, and immaterial exists above the material, natural order.

As twentieth-century history has shown with ghastly consistency, when followed to its logical conclusion, the atheist moral-ethical theory always terminates at the same place: the entrance to Auschwitz.

Chapter Eight

The Atheist Abolition of Man

Not just science but our own other reflections have told us that there is nothing remaining to be explained that could only be explained by the existence of a supreme being, creator or first cause. The universe, and our lives too, all operate exactly as one would expect them to if there were no such thing. So why does the delusion persist?[89]

— Christopher Hitchens

I think, therefore I am.

Even those who are otherwise unfamiliar with the philosopher René Descartes know his famous Latin dictum: *"Cogito, ergo sum"* — *I think, therefore I am*.[90] In just three words, the philosopher described the universally recognized phenomenon of personal consciousness and, in so doing, struck a mortal blow against atheism.

By claiming that only material things exist, atheism renders itself a self-refuting proposition. Ironically, because the atheist denies the existence of anything that is not reducible to material substances, he cannot use ideas, reason, or appeals to logic and remain consistent with his claim. To be consistent, an atheist cannot claim that atheism (or anything else, for that matter) is true, because to assert that he knows something is true necessitates self-awareness, as well as an awareness of ideas that are independent of the self. It would also mean that he is aware that other minds exist.

> You can argue with a man who says, "Rice is unwholesome," but you neither can nor need argue with a man who says, "Rice is unwholesome, but I'm not saying this is true."
> — C. S. Lewis

As C. S. Lewis pointed out, "You can argue with a man who says, 'Rice is unwholesome,' but you neither can nor need argue with a man who says, 'Rice is unwholesome, but I'm not saying this is true.'"

What more needs to be said?

So far, we've seen that atheistic naturalism, were it true, would spell the death of right and wrong, eliminate the possibility of knowledge, and undermine our beliefs in intrinsic human worth and inalienable human rights. But to further illustrate how completely and utterly this worldview fails to account for, and make sense of, our common human experience, in this chapter we take a look at other essential aspects of that common experience — consciousness, individual personality, love, free will, meaning, and purpose.

CONSCIOUSNESS

Naturalist philosopher Geoffrey Maddell admits that "the emergence of consciousness . . . is a mystery, and one to which materialism signally fails to provide an answer."[91]

Similarly, the British philosopher Colin McGinn expresses perplexity at how human consciousness could somehow derive from purely material causes:

> How can mere matter originate consciousness? How did evolution convert the water of biological tissue into the wine of consciousness? Consciousness seems like a radical novelty in the universe, not

prefigured by the after-effects of the Big Bang; so
how did it contrive to spring into being from what
preceded it?[92]

The philosopher Jaegwon Kim, another prominent
naturalist, asks the same question:

> How could a series of physical events — little
> particles jostling one another, electric current
> rushing to and fro, and so on — blossom all of a
> sudden into a conscious experience?[93]

Moreland observes, "Start with matter and tweak it
physically and all you will get is tweaked matter."[94]

Christianity can account for the existence of human
consciousness and personhood on the grounds that God
exists and made human beings in His image and likeness.
It is impossible for atheists, on the other hand, to account
for them on purely natural grounds. "There must be some
natural property that can account for consciousness," they
say, "but we don't yet know what it is. Just as we once could
not scientifically account for things like lightning and
magnetism, in due time scientists will eventually discover
how self-awareness can evolve from an unconscious
material universe composed of particles."

But, just as atheism cannot account coherently for the
existence of the moral law, knowledge, reason, or freedom
of thought, it cannot account for human consciousness and
self-awareness. Atheist apologists such as Greg Epstein
(*Good Without God*), Christopher Hitchens (*God Is Not
Great*), and Richard Dawkins (*The God Delusion*) have,
ironically, demonstrated the logical bankruptcy of atheism
by their theories attempting to explain these phenomena.

Even when atheists are willing to admit that they may never be able to explain human consciousness on a scientific basis, many of those suffering from the Godless delusion nonetheless rest secure in their blind faith and dream of a day to come when science will explain it.

About all a Christian can say to that is, "Dream on."

A breathtaking example of atheism's blind faith can be seen in Ben Stein's eye-opening interview with Richard Dawkins in his movie *Expelled: No Intelligence Allowed.*[95]

STEIN: "Well, who did create the heavens and the earth?"

DAWKINS: "Why do you use the word 'who'? You see, you immediately beg the question by using the word 'who.'"

STEIN: "Well, then how did it get created?"

DAWKINS: "Well, by a very slow process."

STEIN: "Well, how did it start?"

DAWKINS: "Nobody knows how it got started. We know the kind of event that it must have been. We know the sort of event that must have happened for the origin of life."

STEIN: "And what was that?"

DAWKINS: "It was the origin of the first self-replicating molecule."

STEIN: "Right, and how did that happen?"

DAWKINS: "I told you, we don't know."

STEIN: "So you have no idea how it started?"

DAWKINS: "No. Nor does anybody."

STEIN: "What do you think is the possibility that Intelligent Design might turn out to be the answer to some issues in genetics or in Darwinian evolution?"

DAWKINS: "Well, it could come about in the following way. It could be that at some earlier time, somewhere in the universe, a civilization evolved, probably by some kind of Darwinian means, probably to a very, very high level of technology, and designed a form of life that they seeded onto perhaps this planet. Um, now that is a possibility, and an intriguing possibility. And I suppose it's possible that you might find evidence for that if you look at the details of biochemistry, molecular biology, you might find a signature of some sort of designer."

So Richard Dawkins here presents an "aliens from outer space must have done it" explanation for all this.

(Come on, Dr. Dawkins. Space aliens? *Seriously*?)

The atheist says, "Because naturalism is true, there must, therefore, be a scientific explanation for the existence of human consciousness."

The Christian responds, "Isn't it *possible* that the inability of naturalism to account for human consciousness is evidence that naturalism is *not* true? That there's more to this universe than particles in motion? What if the *truth* is that God's existence, and our creation in God's image, *is* what accounts for human consciousness? Wouldn't you want to know the truth, if that was in fact the truth?"

"It cannot be the truth."

"Why not?"

"Because I am a scientist, and as a scientist I believe only what can be observed and measured by the use of the scientific method. To use the scientific method, I have to assume that the natural world is all that exists and that there is a natural explanation for everything, including human consciousness. If I open the door to even the possibility of God's existence as the explanation for consciousness, then I am no longer a scientist but a theologian. Non-natural explanations cannot be allowed."

"But again," the Christian asks, "what if the truth is that there is no natural explanation for human consciousness because God exists, and He created us with self-awareness and consciousness? What if the tweaking of matter can never explain human consciousness? In this case, wouldn't your insistence on natural explanations be leading you *away from* the truth? It begins to sound as if you aren't so much interested in finding the truth as you are in finding natural explanations for everything."

"That's because naturalism is true."

> It could be that at some earlier time, somewhere in the universe, a civilization evolved, probably by some kind of Darwinian means, probably to a very, very high level of technology, and designed a form of life that they seeded onto perhaps this planet.
>
> — Richard Dawkins

INDIVIDUAL PERSONALITY AND EMOTIONS

What about individual personality? What would personality *be* in a materialist universe?

Our experience is that people have complex and uniquely individual personalities. They have their own way of thinking and relating, their own sense of humor, their own likes and dislikes, abilities, desires, loves. And none of us believes that what we see and experience in the personalities of our friends and family can be accounted for by merely talking about electrochemical reactions in a brain.

In fact, our commonsense perception is that people are precisely what the Christian worldview teaches that they are — individual souls — and that their personalities and expressions of emotion are expressions of their souls.

Kenneth writes:

> I think back to when my daughter Blythe was very young, and then my son Kenny was born. It was obvious from the beginning that each came into this world his or her own person. Even though born into the same essential environment, and from the same parents, they were different in a million ways and from the very beginning.
>
> And they have maintained to this day the essential personalities that were evident from the start.
>
> And now my wife and I have two beautiful granddaughters, Hero (the beautiful and pure damsel from Shakespeare's *Much Ado About Nothing*) and Mary (take a wild guess). In these two, we see exactly the same thing once again.

Hero and Mary are two distinct persons with two distinct personalities. Mary is a two-year-old Annie Oakley. She *stands* on the back of the rocking horse while holding the reins.

Hero cares about nothing but dressing up like Cinderella or her favorite, Sleeping Beauty (pronounced "Sheepin Booie") and prancing around the house.

Yesterday Hero went to the pediatrician for her third-year checkup. Wanting to make some light conversation, the doctor asked her, "So Hero, what is your favorite food?"

To which she replied, "Sheepin Booie food."

"Oh, really," he said, "and what kind of food is that?"

"Wine!" she returned, with an attitude of *Duh, you're a doctor and you don't know that?*

I wonder. What would my daughter and son and granddaughters *be* if atheism were true? The unique ways in which they think, perceive, enjoy, relate, experience, smile, laugh, speak — what would this be if there were no spirit in them and they were not human souls?

Francis Crick has ventured an answer to that question:

You, your joys and your sorrows, your memories and your ambitions, your sense of personal identity and free will, are in fact *no more than* the behavior of a vast assembly of nerve cells and their associated molecules.

Crick's philosophy, then, effectively reduces human beings from a *who* to a *what*: what we know as someone's "personality" is nothing more than his body's biochemistry and molecular activity.[96]

If atheism is true and God does not exist, then human beings are not "persons" in any sense that transcends a particular collection of molecules. We are, instead, merely "biochemical machines" with particular quirks of behavior we call "personalities" that are just the result of brain activity.

Ultimately, the atheist worldview — when taken to its absurd logical conclusions — results in the abolition of man.

LOVE

Atheists like to boast about their compassion, tolerance, solidarity, and "love" for their fellow human beings. But what would "love" be in an atheist universe?[97] Certainly not love as all of us know and experience it.

Love is a universal human experience that declares the truth: human beings are more than just "evolved matter." Most of us love many people and are loved by many people. At the very least, everyone loves at least *someone,* and very few people don't have the experience of someone else loving *them*. It's no surprise, therefore, that because love is such a profound, powerful, and life-changing human reality, countless poems, sonnets, and songs have been composed in an effort to express the inexpressible — what it feels to love and be loved, to love and have one's love ignored or rejected, and so on.

While it may not be true, strictly speaking, that "all you need is love," it is undeniably true that everyone everywhere *loves* love and has a deep and abiding desire to love and be loved.

But why?

Love is diffusive and expresses itself in myriad ways — none of them explicable on a purely naturalist basis. You know this because you, like everyone, have experienced this many times. But what is it that makes us willing to risk our own lives — even to the point of sacrificing them — to protect a wife, children, family, friends, communities, and country?

Clearly, the bleak universe of atheism simply cannot account for love. Atheists can appeal to the exigencies of neurons and brain chemistry all they want, but to no avail. Science cannot explain love.

Patrick writes about how he felt when he first met his future wife, Nancy:

> She was sixteen and I was seventeen when I met her. Slim, lovely, and always smiling, Nancy was one of those vivid young women people instinctively like and want to be around. For a year and a half, we were just friends, and we dated other people. We often saw each other casually, and I sometimes even played bass for the parish choir she sang in. When the relationship with my girlfriend fizzled, I got my nerve up to ask Nancy on a date.
>
> The next year was a blur of happy times spent with Nancy: long walks on the beach, bike rides, holding hands and talking for hours, playing Frisbee,

laughing, quiet moments gazing at the stars on warm summer nights.

She was fantastic and wonderful, alive in a deeper and more attractive way than any girl I had ever known. She was Catholic and beautiful, and I loved being with her. Best of all, Nancy never allowed herself to get caught up in any of the typical teenage vices, and that was immensely attractive to me.

I was drawn by her radiant goodness as much as her physical beauty and sweet, loving personality. She amazed me with a wisdom and depth of vitality that was beyond anything I had to offer her. She loved with chaste yet stirring intensity. Her love was a current of goodness that was wide, deep, and unstoppable, the way a mountain stream surges onward to find its waterfall. I came to realize that I loved her.[98]

What exactly did Patrick fall in love with? Was it the unique combination of cells and neurons and chemical reactions that formed a pretty young woman called "Nancy?" On the other hand, what man in his right mind would — or even *could* — fall in love with a woman-shaped "collection of cells"? The notion is absurd.

No. Patrick fell in love with the *person* Nancy. She, like any human being, is something more than just a sum of parts, more than the collection of atoms that make up her body. She has a mind, personality, knowledge, dreams, and memories. Nancy has the capacity to love and to be loved. And none of those qualities is material; they are all spiritual. *They,* not a complex combination of atoms —

however pleasingly arranged — are what men and women see and fall in love with.

Love, like personhood and self-awareness, cannot be reducible to atoms, and a "person" is not merely a complete collection of body parts. Just ask someone who has lost a limb in war or an accident. His legs may be gone, but who he is as a *person* remains fully intact.

What is it that makes us willing to risk our own lives — even to the point of sacrificing them — to protect a wife, children, family, friends, communities, and country?

Atheism's narrow, strictly material worldview cannot account for *love*. It cannot account for *personhood* — the most basic, universally recognized human reality.

The Christian theistic worldview, however, can. Easily. Effortlessly.

Why? Because, as a very old book once said, "God is love."

What about the love human beings have for beauty of all sorts? Ask yourself: Why do our hearts respond excitedly and gratefully, as they do, to beauty? How is it that we can even *recognize* beauty as beauty? The sight of the sun breaking gloriously through the clouds after a heavy rain, the azure blue sky above and all the world beneath washed clean and new — why does this affect us as it does? The movement of a particularly beautiful musical piece,[99] even the sound of an oboe holding a single note, "high and unwavering," as the Austrian court composer, Salieri, described it with intense feeling in the film *Amadeus* — why does any of this have the ability to flood our hearts with love and joy, or sometimes even loneliness and sadness?

Atheists will claim that the only thing that really matters is the ability of living organisms to adapt to their environment, flourish, and reproduce in large numbers. If that is true, then, on what *purely natural* basis can we account for the fact that human beings possess so many attributes and aspirations that go so far beyond what random genetic mutation would tend to produce? Why do we human beings compose music and write poetry? Why do we write novels? Why do we engage in painting, illustration, and dance? Why do many find the study of abstract things such as history, culture, philosophy, and languages so fulfilling? Why do we explore the sciences? Why do we seek the answers to abstract and complex mathematical questions that have no material presence in the natural world, that no one has ever seen, and that, for all we know, have no practical application? Why do we love and pursue knowledge for its own sake?

None of this makes sense if, as atheists do, you base your worldview on the premise that we are nothing more than products of nature. We don't see any of these qualities in nature. But we do see them, profoundly so, in human nature. What's more, they appear to be utterly transcendent. But how?

Even more mysterious, on naturalist grounds, is how we humans seem to positively yearn for things that *would not exist at all* were naturalism true.

C. S. Lewis once remarked that we cannot imagine a fish that has lived its entire existence under water naturally evolving a burning desire to live on dry ground and breathe air, or to fly like a bird in the sky. It's fair to assume at that point that a species existing within an environment doesn't evolve the desire for something that doesn't even *exist* in that environment. And yet we who — according to the atheist worldview — exist *within* an entirely natural environment and have no experience of any other environment somehow yearn for God, for heaven, and for eternal life.

> If atheism was true, then Mozart is lucky he died before learning the awful reality: that his musical genius was meaningless.

Human beings throughout history have believed in God and longed for eternity — neither of which could exist if naturalism is true.[100] On the other hand, if the Christian theistic worldview is true, then love is something far more than chemistry. It is real, spiritual, and irreducible to matter.

Poor Mozart. If atheism is true, then the maestro is lucky he died before learning the awful reality: that his musical genius was meaningless, simply the result of an accidental excess of neurons firing aimlessly away in his brain. And the love and admiration that millions have felt for his music are also essentially meaningless.

But whatever naturalists might *say* about such things, they *live* as though love, music, truth, and beauty are more than mere "brain chemistry." Oh, yes. Atheists have written and will continue to write poetry; admire works of art; compose music; and love their families and friends. They regard the love of others for them as more than something merely physical or emotionally pleasurable. They value love for its own sake, not just because someone's love for them makes them feel good. Atheists recognize, as we all do, that love *itself* is good. And there's the rub. But how can an atheist rationally, consistently value things such as love, truth, and beauty for their own sakes, when — in strict atheist doctrinal terms — they do not really exist in themselves?

Most God-deniers are as likely as Christians are to get a little choked up at the sight of the television news footage of coal miners rescued and reunited with their families after being trapped underground for three days.[101] Why is this? Because even atheists know that love is more than just a chemical reaction in the brain.

Behold the wondrously bizarre dichotomy of the "Godless delusion."

- In order to defend his claim that only material things exist, the atheist must deny the existence of anything immaterial.

- But, as his moment-to-moment actions reveal, the atheist's daily life is pervaded by immaterial realities such as love, truth, beauty, goodness, and knowledge, upon which he must rely for his life to have any meaning.

It's a thoroughly unenviable predicament, one that can only be summarized by the old adage some parents say to their children: "Do as I say, not as I do."

FREE WILL

Free will fares no better than love in an atheist universe. According to the commonsense understanding of the terms "freedom" and "free will," we say that a person acts "freely" only if his or her "choices" aren't determined ahead of time. Another way to speak of free will is *intentionality*. Human beings are intentional in their thoughts and actions. We do things and think things for a reason.

Atheist philosopher John Searle has admitted that this common notion of freedom is so inescapable that even if it is an illusion, given the physical determinism inherent in a naturalist universe, we would have to live as though it were not. He comments that when dining in a fine restaurant and presented by the waiter with a choice between pork and veal, it's not a viable option to reply, "Look, I'm a determinist. I will just have to wait to see what order happens!"[102]

The concept of free will is rooted in our universal experience. You are free to put this book down at this instant and stop reading it. You are free to pause and think about what you plan to do tomorrow.

FREEDOM TO CHOOSE THE GOOD

By free will, [man] is capable of directing himself toward his true good. He finds his perfection "in seeking and loving what is true and good" (*Gaudium et Spes*, 15§2).

Freedom is the power, rooted in reason and will, to act or not to act, to do this or that, and so to perform deliberate actions on one's own responsibility. By free will one shapes one's own life. Human freedom is a force for growth and maturity in truth and goodness; it attains its perfection when directed toward God, our beatitude.

— *Catechism of the Catholic Church* 1704, 1731

Each of us is aware — immediately and intuitively — that we have the free will to choose to eat chicken or veal, apples or oranges, Mexican enchiladas or Irish stew. Daily life is comprised of a succession of free-will choices. Some of our choices are influenced by external forces beyond our control: paying taxes, for example. But, aside from the relatively few compulsory "choices" we make, we determine our own actions based on our free will. They are not predetermined for us.

This is perfectly consistent with the theistic worldview: Christian moral principles, complete with responsibility and accountability, rest on the foundation of free will. If you are not free to choose good or evil, if you are compelled by an external force to do something against your will, you cannot be culpable for that action. Any woman who has been raped cannot be held "accountable" for an act she was forced to endure and had no freedom to avoid.

But free will is completely inexplicable when considered from the standpoint of the materialist worldview.

As John Searle admits:

> [W]e are inclined to say that since nature consists of particles and their relations with each other, and since everything can be accounted for in terms of those particles and their relations, there is simply no room for freedom of will. . . . It really does look as if everything we know about physics forces us to some form of denial of human freedom.[103]

Physical systems are deterministic. Machines move as their parts determine. The eight ball always goes precisely where it is determined to go, given the angle, velocity, and "spin" of the cue ball. Since the naturalist worldview says that the universe represents one massive physical system, it is deterministic — even with respect to the human mind, the thoughts it has, and the choices it makes. (Even the arguments of Dawkins and Hitchens are predetermined!)

But if this is true, then why write? Why speak? Why debate? If all our thoughts and actions are predetermined, then why bother choose one career over another or one woman over another to marry? Why even bother to get up in the morning?

And why treat addicts and criminals as though they were accountable for their actions? In a naturalistic world, both the alcoholic and the child molester are equally "determined" to do the things they do by forces outside their control. Neither can be held "responsible" for his actions. So why does poor Bernie Madoff, one of the biggest swindlers of all time, have to spend the rest of his life in prison? Didn't forces beyond his control push him to create the Ponzi scheme that defrauded investors of several billion-with-a-b dollars?

Perhaps Madoff's defense attorney could have invoked the "particles and their relations" defense. He could have brought in expert atheist philosophers such as John Searle to testify that since "everything can be accounted for in terms of particles and their relations," whatever the defendant may have done was entirely predetermined. He could have further explained that the laws his client is supposed to have broken were determined entirely by "particles and their relations" in the brains of various legislators. And in his closing statement (determined, of course, by "particles and their relations" in his own brain), our free-thinking naturalist attorney could have reminded the jurors that as they retired to the deliberation room, they should keep firmly in mind that their votes for either a guilty or not-guilty verdict also will be determined by "particles and their relations" in their individual brains. The same would be true of the judge's sentence.

AN EXERCISE IN DENIAL

> As if in some kind of metaphysical clearance sale, the atheist announces that "everything must go!"

Naturalism *requires* a denial of the existence of an absolute standard of right and wrong. It recognizes the existence of the brain but must deny the existence of the mind. It must deny the intrinsic, transcendent value and dignity of human beings ("A rat is a pig is a dog is a boy. They are all mammals"— remember?). It must dismiss human consciousness, personality, and love as "particles and their relations." And now, when pushed to still further absurd conclusions, naturalism necessarily entails a denial of human free will and moral accountability as well.

As if in some kind of metaphysical clearance sale, the atheist announces that "everything must go!" Why? Because none of what makes human beings *human* remotely fits into his material-only view of the universe.

The naturalist worldview is 100 percent vulnerable to the *reductio ad absurdum* that dogs every step an atheist takes in his denial of the existence of God. Say what he may, the logical implications of the atheist's denials are absurd.

Perhaps *the* crowning ignominy of the Godless delusion is that it cannot account for the freedom of thought required for atheists to derive their worldview at all, much less argue for it.

MEANING

Finally, let's consider how atheism attempts to account for something as basic as meaning in human life. What would happen to the concept of "meaning" in an atheist-naturalist universe?

Yeah, you guessed it. Meaning would *have* no meaning.

Christians believe that God created the cosmos and everything in it for a purpose. Philosophers speak of purpose as the *teleology*[104] of any given thing. An eye's purpose is to see; a hammer's purpose is to pound. A honeybee's purpose is to buzz around gathering nectar, building a hive where it can store it, pollinate plants along the way, and reproduce.

The Christian worldview shares certain fundamental truths that were first explained by Aristotle. In his book *The Last Superstition*, Catholic philosopher Edward Feser discusses Aristotle's view of these matters of nature, purpose, and meaning. According to Aristotle, a squirrel (Feser's illustration) possesses a particular *nature* — its "squirrelness," let's say. Its *purpose* is to "instantiate" that nature — to be an instance of that nature, to exemplify "squirrelness" — in short, to be a squirrel. Thus, according to Aristotle, a squirrel could be said to be a "good squirrel," a squirrel that is fulfilling its "purpose," to the extent that it most perfectly instantiates its "squirrelness."

Feser explains:

> Hence a squirrel who likes to scamper up trees and gather nuts for the winter (or whatever) is going to be a more perfect approximation of the squirrel essence than one which, through habituation or genetic defect, prefers to eat toothpaste spread on Ritz crackers and to lay out "spread eagled" on the freeway. This entails a standard of goodness and a perfectly objective one.[105]

For Aristotle, a good squirrel is a squirrel that scampers up trees and stores nuts for the winter. A squirrel that spends its days spread-eagled on the freeway, eating toothpaste on crackers, would not be a "good squirrel" in that it is not instantiating the nature of *squirrelness* very well. It's not pursuing the end for which it was created. It's not directed toward its goal.

Christianity holds that God created human beings in His image and likeness to instantiate His nature and character. He designed humankind in general, and each individual person in particular, for a purpose: to "know, love, and serve God in this life and to be happy with Him in the life to come"[106] — *and*, along the way, to be and to become (in every respect appropriate to man as a creature) the image and likeness of God. As men and women strive, by God's grace — in their characters, their relationships, and their lives — to be like Him, they fulfill the purpose for which they were created. Therefore, this life has a transcendent meaning that goes beyond the particular circumstances in which any given person finds himself or herself.

And so, St. Paul encourages the believers in Ephesus, "Therefore be imitators of God, as beloved children. And walk in love, as Christ loved us and gave himself up for us" (Eph. 5:1-2). In his letter to the Romans, he speaks of the goal of human redemption as being that men and women might be "conformed to the image of his [God's] Son" (8:29). This is what we're made for, so it shouldn't be surprising to find that those who pursue this purpose with all their hearts report that joy, peace, and fulfillment are what you encounter when you venture along this path.

No Meaning

Naturalism, by contrast, is not a teleological worldview. It says: Man was not created; he has no "nature." He just *is*. Man has no purpose. He's just *here*. Man's life has no overarching meaning. His existence here is an accident. As Jean-Paul Sartre was fond of saying, "Existence precedes essence." In other words, we are not born with some "nature" that we are to instantiate. Each one of us appears on the scene alive, accidents of a soulless material universe. We are free to decide for ourselves what we will be and what our purpose in life, if any, will be.

Thus, an objective human "nature," "purpose," or "meaning" is out the window. Instead, man is free to be and do whatever he wants. He is free to strive after whatever goals his appetites draw him toward. He is free to find whatever "meaning" he can come up with to somehow satisfy his innate desire for meaning.

What about meaning as far as the universe is concerned? Well, there is none. The universe just *is*. It's a cosmos comprised of neutral, brute facts. And its history, as someone once said, is "just one damned thing after another."

In the words of atheist apologist Bertrand Russell:

> Man is the product of causes which had no provision for the end they were achieving; his origin, his growth, his hopes and fears, his loves and beliefs, are but the outcome of accidental collisions of atoms; no fire, no intensity of thought and feeling can preserve the individual life beyond the grave; all the labor of the ages, all the devotion, all the inspiration, all the noonday brightness of human genius, are destined to extinction in the vast death of the solar system.[107]

Sartre expressed the utter meaninglessness of human existence in a Godless universe:

> Death is the final absurdity which befittingly finishes off what the final absurdity of birth began.[108]

Not surprisingly, one of Sartre's most famous books was titled *No Exit.*

The late Harvard evolutionist Stephen Jay Gould stated naturalism's denial of meaning about as bluntly as it could be stated. In answer to the question "Why are we here?", he responded:

> We are here because one odd group of fishes had a particular fin anatomy that could transform into legs for terrestrial creatures; because the earth never froze entirely during the Ice Age; because a small and tenuous species, arising in Africa a quarter of a million years ago, has managed, so far, to survive by hook and by crook. We may yearn for a higher answer — but none exists.[109]

Now, the Titanic of Western civilization has collided with the iceberg of the Godless delusion, which has ripped an enormous gash in civilization's hull. Our society is progressively being flooded with the cold, dark waters of atheism, and we're sinking. The further we drift, crippled by the water-logging effects of naturalism, the less likely it is that those in the lifeboats will be able to find and collect the passengers who are thrashing around in the water. Much less will they be able to convince those who stubbornly remain on the deck of the doomed ship that if only they would get into the lifeboats, they would be saved.

And yet, the band plays on.

> We are here because one odd group of fishes had a particular fin anatomy that could transform into legs for terrestrial creatures . . . We may yearn for a higher answer — but none exists.
>
> — Stephen Jay Gould

The result of all this bleak meaninglessness, on the one hand, is that modern man finds himself lost in a purposeless, material universe. On the other hand, he finds himself free to be and do whatever he wants and to live by whatever standards he chooses. It is, ironically, a freedom of ultimate meaninglessness. It is a sense of a despairing "lostness" conjoined with a sense of boundless freedom.

Most often, in fact, the two seem to come as a package, the one reinforcing the other. Modern man's sense of lostness leads him to the exercise of boundless freedom in search of meaning and happiness; and the exercise of boundless freedom — because he is created for something better and higher — leads to an ever more profound sense of lostness. (For illustration, ask any forty-year-old single man or woman who was led to believe that they would find happiness in unbounded sexual freedom.)

Christians point out that this sense of lostness will only deepen as modern man turns away from living according to his purpose. Thus, if you have the stomach for it, do a Google search for bizarre surgeries that people undergo to make themselves resemble lions or reptiles. Seriously. Or explore the Internet for the weddings of those who marry trees and inanimate objects. There are many even worse things — horrifying things — that are also going on out there. We do not recommend you Google-search for them.

If a man who had perfect eyesight were to decide that he was really a "blind man trapped in the body of a man with sight," and if he proceeded to have his eyes surgically removed so that he could "truly be himself," you would know he is suffering from some extreme emotional and psychological problems. He'd be institutionalized as fast as you could say, "Squirrels don't eat toothpaste."

But then, if atheism is true and God does not exist — if the naturalist worldview is correct, and the universe is a big, busy, ultimately meaningless place in which we each have the freedom to define our own essence and establish our own standards of behavior — then the crazy man who has his eyes removed so he can be "who he really is" isn't really crazy at all. Nor is the man who makes himself into a reptile, or the woman who pledges her troth to a sycamore tree. All these are just acting consistently with the absurd logical conclusions required if atheism were true.

Happily, it's not true.

Some atheists claim to have no problem with human life having no purpose or meaning. They conclude that having no ultimate purpose does not fatally cripple one's ability to find some kind of temporal "meaning," such as possessions, achievements, friends, and lovers. But there is good evidence that the atheist's subjectivizing of such things has a decidedly negative effect on society. Naturalism leads to a position not unlike that of the Sophists of the Greek period. As W. T. Jones writes:

> Though it is certainly impossible to make an absolutely firm judgment, there are grounds for holding that subjectivity and naturalism have a deleterious effect on culture. The view of value to which modern science seem to commit us is in many respects similar to that of the Greek Sophists. Greek Sophism was certainly accompanied by a general insensitivity to values, by a concentration on pleasure as the sole good, and by a radically egocentric morality.[110]

Based squarely on atheist beliefs, the most evil totalitarian regimes have arisen, regimes in which the worth of the individual meant nothing whatsoever. But even on a personal level, we see a drifting away from self-respect, self-control, modesty, honesty, humility, and gentleness.

If God does not exist — and if all that does exist is a vast universe of purely natural beings that have for eons been jostling one another in an endless, random, evolutionary struggle for the survival of the fittest — then why be anything other than a greedy, consuming, self-centered bundle of appetites and emotions? "Might makes right." Right? If it feels good, do it. Right? Get what you can get, as long as you can get it, from whomever you can get. Right?

If you are an atheist, the only answer you can give is, "Right."

But if you believe in God, you know that the real answer to all of this is, "Yeah, *right*."

CHAPTER NINE

OF RANCHERS AND RUSTLERS

Have you not heard of that madman who lit a lantern in the bright morning hours, ran to the marketplace and cried incessantly, "I'm looking for God, I'm looking for God!" As many of those who did not believe in God were standing together there, he excited considerable laughter. "Why, did he get lost?" said one. "Did he lose his way like a child?" said another. "Or is he hiding? Is he afraid of us? Has he gone on a voyage? Or emigrated?" Thus they yelled and laughed. The madman sprang into their midst and pierced them with his eyes. "Whither is God?" he cried. "I shall tell you. We have killed him — you and I. All of us are his murderers. But how have we done this? How were we able to drink up the sea? Who gave us the sponge to wipe away the entire horizon? What did we do when we unchained this earth from its sun? Whither is it moving now? Whither are we moving now? Away from all sides? Are we not plunging continually backward, sideward, forward, in all directions? Is there an up or down left? Are we not straying as through an infinite nothing? Do we not feel the breath of empty space? Has it not become colder? Is not night and more night coming on all the time?"

— Friedrich Nietzsche[111]

In his *Parable of The Madman*, Nietzsche, often called the "father of modern atheism," paints a disturbing image of the implications of the intellectual revolution taking place throughout Western civilization during his lifetime.

His "madman" lights a lantern and runs through the streets announcing to the townspeople that, having effectively murdered God and banished him from the universe, they must now accept and expect a world of infinite emptiness and meaninglessness. *Are we not straying through an infinite nothing? Do we not feel the*

*breath of empty space? Has it not become colder? Is not
night and more night coming all the time?* Certainly, since
God is dead, men and women will now be free to think
and act for themselves — but in Nietzsche's parable, all
the madman can see, all he can speak of, is the darkness
that lies ahead.

The God-murdering madman, with lantern in hand,
foretells the future and, like a biblical prophet, warns
of what is to come upon the earth as a result of the new
conditions inherent in a world without God.

It's not a pretty picture.

Atheist philosopher John Searle asks himself and
modern naturalists the key question of our modern age:

> There is exactly one overriding question in
> contemporary philosophy . . . How do we fit in? . . .
> How can we square this self-conception of ourselves
> as mindful, meaning-creating, free, rational, etc.,
> agents with a universe that consists entirely of
> mindless, meaningless, un-free, non-rational, brute
> physical particles? [112]

This is precisely the question with which we challenge
atheists in this book: How can the naturalist square the
universal intuitive conception we have of ourselves, based
on our universal commonsense experience, with what he
tells us about the nature of the world in which we live?

We are self-aware. The naturalist universe is mindless.

We perceive meaning everywhere. The naturalist
universe is meaningless.

We are free. The naturalist universe is hopelessly deterministic.

We are rational. The naturalist universe is comprised from top to bottom of impersonal and non-rational, brute physical particles.

We see human beings as *persons* possessing intrinsic worth and human dignity. The naturalist universe is value-neutral.

We believe in human rights. The naturalist universe knows nothing of rights. Whatever exists is natural, and whatever is natural is . . . well, it just *is*.

If it were not for the deep religious commitment naturalists have to the worldview of naturalism, wouldn't this be sufficient evidence that naturalism isn't true — the fact that it is unable to begin to explain or account for the most basic, essential, and pervasive aspects of human experience? As we've seen in quotation after quotation, atheists readily admit that morality, the mind, reason, human worth, free will, and value seem to flatly contradict the naturalist worldview.

How does a naturalist or modern-day atheist even square his ability to think through and state his position "with a universe that consists entirely of mindless, meaningless, un-free, non-rational, brute physical particles?"

Understandably, most atheists object to this line of thinking.

> How can we square this self-conception of ourselves as mindful, meaning-creating, free, rational, etc., agents with a universe that consists entirely of mindless, meaningless, un-free, non-rational, brute physical particles?
>
> — John Searle

For instance, some argue, "Sure, it may be difficult to explain the human mind or free will in terms of naturalism. But we simply have to deal with reality. Hasn't science already demonstrated a naturalist worldview to be true?"

Not in the least.

As was mentioned in an earlier chapter, this isn't a question science can answer. Within the branches of philosophy, it is metaphysics that grapples with the question, "What is the nature of reality?" and epistemology that asks, "How do we know?" or "What is the basis for knowledge?" As Aristotle said, these are "above" the physical sciences such as chemistry and biology, which are limited to the study of the material world. The questions of whether naturalism is true, or whether God exists and a supernatural and immaterial or spiritual world exists as well — these questions are inherently philosophical, not scientific, in nature.

The methods science uses to study the natural world — empirical observation, the development of possible explanatory hypotheses (all of them natural), and experimentation to test these various hypotheses — apply only to what can be seen, heard, smelled, tasted, and touched. So, since God, angels, and human souls would all be invisible and spiritual in nature rather than visible and material, the fact that no scientist has seen them in his microscope or telescope doesn't "prove" that they don't exist; it *can't* prove anything of the sort.

Nor can the "truth" of naturalism be proven merely because scientists using the scientific method, employing scientific instruments, and conducting scientific experiments — all designed for the study of the natural and material universe — find only a natural, material universe.

Faith and Reason

Though faith is above reason, there can never be any real discrepancy between faith and reason. Since the same God who reveals mysteries and infuses faith has bestowed the light of reason on the human mind, God cannot deny himself, nor can truth ever contradict truth. . . . The humble and persevering investigator of the secrets of nature is being led, as it were, by the hand of God in spite of himself, for it is God, the conserver of all things, who made them what they are.

— *Catechism of the Catholic Church* 159

This will likely come as a surprise to most atheists. In their haste to lay claim to the scientific "high ground" (the preferred launching platform from which they rain down endless salvos of supposed scientific refutations of theism), atheists have overlooked one important detail. Science is utterly incapable of answering the question, "Does God exist?" Atheists may be very competent scientists, but they are lousy metaphysicians. They have hit the bull's-eye on the wrong target.

The "Scientific Fact" That . . . Isn't

So if modern science hasn't demonstrated naturalism to be true, how is it that scientists operate on the assumption that it is "fact"?

Good question.

Christian philosopher Dallas Willard takes up this very issue in an article titled *Knowledge and Naturalism*.[113] He points out that naturalism is exactly that — an *assumption* of modern science. It is something modern naturalists simply believe, not something anyone has demonstrated or could demonstrate scientifically.

He explains that, while there are a number of scientific fields, and each has its own subject matter and particular methodology (e.g. chemistry, astronomy, physics, mathematics, biology, anatomy, geology), "None of them has as their subject matter *reality as a whole* or *knowledge as a whole*." For good reason: these are the proper subject matter of metaphysics and epistemology.

Willard then argues further that there *could be no science* that could determine the overall nature of reality.

> [M]odern naturalism is often specified simply in terms of an exclusive application of scientific method in all inquiries. But how can this method *support claims about the nature of reality as a whole?* For example, one might state that the only realities are atoms (quarks, strings, etc.) and derivatives thereof. But how is he to support his claim? It certainly cannot be derived from any specific science (physics, chemistry on up) or from any conjunction of specific sciences. And it is not to be

dcrived through any application of experimental techniques within any science.

Because of this, Willard explains, modern thought most often simply falls back on the abstraction of "Science," stipulating that "science" has somehow "demonstrated" that nothing exists but the world that science is studying — the physical world. Note that the word *stipulate* means to "lay down as a condition of an agreement." Naturalism is something many modern scientists lay down as agreed upon, just one of the presupposed "ground rules" for engaging in scientific inquiry.

This modern approach to science — indeed, to the theory of knowledge itself — is the natural byproduct of the attack on classical metaphysics by two key Enlightenment philosophers: David Hume (1711-1776) and Emmanuel Kant (1724-1804). Hume argued for empiricism, meaning that human beings cannot know anything except for what can be encountered directly by the senses. Kant proposed that nothing can really be said to have intrinsic "meaning" apart from the "meaning" which human beings, individually and collectively, impose on the world around them. In other words, neither the cosmos nor anything contained within it possesses any objective meaning, but remains unintelligible until man subjectively imposes meaning.[114]

But Willard continues:

> John Searle seems to be in this position. He speaks of "our scientific view of the world," which according to him every informed person with her wits about her now believes to be true. He speaks of a view of the

world which includes "all of our generally accepted theories about what sort of place the universe is and how it works." "It includes," he continues, "theories ranging from quantum mechanics and relativity theory to the plate tectonic theory of geology and the DNA theory of hereditary transmission,"[115] etc.

But this will hardly do what he wants.... Such specific scientific theories as those just mentioned — and no matter how many of them we may list — cannot provide an ontology [a theory of "being," of "what exists"]. They never even attempt to determine what it is to exist or what existence is, and cannot by the nature of their content provide an exhaustive list of what ultimate sorts of things there are....

In support of this claim, we ask: Could one possibly find the place in some comprehensive and duly accredited scientific text or treatment, or some technical paper, where it is demonstrated or necessarily assumed by the science concerned that all that exists consists of particles or fields or strings — or whatever the proper subject matter of the science is? Would Searle or anyone else be able to mention the name of the physicist who established this as an "obvious fact of physics"? Exactly where in the "atomic theory of matter" is the claim about what "the universe consists entirely of" to be found?

"After all," Searle rhetorically asks, "do we not know from the discoveries of science that there is really nothing in the universe but physical particles and fields of forces acting on physical particles?" The answer, contrary to his assumption, is "No, we do not." Again, could he possibly just point out when, where, how, and by whom this "discovery of science" was made. Was it made?

SUCCESS = PROOF?

Naturalism (sometimes referred to as physicalism[116]) is presented as though it were a proven fact of science because science has succeeded in illuminating so many things in our world. Then the question arises, "Don't the undeniable successes of modern science justify the belief that the naturalist worldview is true?"

Again . . . no, they do not. In fact, this isn't an argument at all.

Think about it. A Christian theist can study the natural world and discover anything a naturalist can discover. Believers have made hugely important advances in medicine, engineering, physics, chemistry, biology, and many more fields. In fact, many scientists who believe in God have for centuries stood at the forefront of cutting-edge scientific inquiry, literally for as long as "science" has been around. And they continue to do so. So having studied the natural world and found success in solving practical scientific problems does not, by definition, mean that science, or the natural world, "is all there is."

The point here is *not* to engage in a foolish and pointless "My dad can beat up your dad" type of comparison between theist and atheist scientists. Rather, it is to underscore the fact that doing science well does not lead one inevitably to embrace a naturalist worldview. In fact, the indisputable successes of science have no logical connection whatsoever with the atheist argument (really, more of a "wild leap") that "all that exists is the natural world."

At best, the atheist is, yet again, caught in a circular argument: "Science has proven that God — a non-physical being — does not exist because science can find no physical evidence to support the possibility of his existence."

Patrick recounts a humorous story floating around the Internet in which an atheist discovers how silly that kind of "reasoning" is when trying to refute a believer.

A college student was in a philosophy class, which had a discussion about God's existence. The professor presented the following logic:

"Has anyone in this class ever heard God?" Nobody spoke.

"Has anyone in this class ever touched God?" Again, nobody spoke.

"Has anyone in this class ever seen God?"

When, for the third time, nobody answered, he declared to the class, "Then there is no God."

One student thought about this for a minute and then raised his hand to ask a question. The teacher called on him, and he stood and asked his classmates:

"Has anyone in this class heard our professor's brain?" Silence.

"Has anyone in this class ever touched the professor's brain?" Absolute silence.

"Has anyone in this class ever seen the professor's brain?"

The class remained silent. After a few moments, the student announced to everyone, "Then, according to the professor's own logic, it must be true that he has no brain."

If only the debate with atheists over God's existence were as simple and humorous as that! Their arguments against God are silly, typically wrapped within the impressive trappings of science, and about as effective as the poor fictional college professor's benighted logic.

The "science says!" mantra, so popular with modern atheists, is either a purposeful sleight-of-hand or an embarrassing intellectual gaffe that otherwise intelligent people should do their best to avoid. Which brings to mind Thomas Dolby's 1982 hit song, *She Blinded Me with Science.*[117] We're pretty confident he wasn't intentionally mocking the "science says!" credulity inherent in atheist-naturalism . . . but he surely could have been.

To borrow and refashion a turn of a phrase from the "other camp":

Atheists will never accept that we theists have the better argument. They just pester us and waste our time with their arguments from "science," as if that proved anything.

Of course, some naturalism is necessary in scientific thought. A scientist who would seriously propose, for example, that "fairies" make the leaves turn yellow in autumn would likely not pursue the question far enough to discover the real reason leaves turn yellow — the scientific reason. Bringing "God" into the picture *in that fashion* derails scientific investigation.

Understood.

But the converse is also true: If God exists, there just *might not be a natural explanation for everything.*

What if the universe we live in is more like the universe the Christian theist believes it is? What if God exists, and the real world is comprised of material as well as non-material realities? What if the mind is not identical to, and interchangeable with, the brain? What if God's existence and our creation in God's image *is* what accounts for free will, self-consciousness, personality, and all the rest? What then?

> By *assuming* at the outset the truth of naturalism, modern science winds up being not a search for the truth but a search for natural explanations of things.

Surely, most people expect that science should be the unflinching, courageous, and systematic search for the truth of things, whatever that truth may be. By *assuming* at the outset the truth of naturalism, however, modern science winds up being not a search for the truth but a search for natural explanations of things. And the two are not synonymous.

But this doesn't matter to the naturalist. Even when a firm insistence on "natural explanations only" results in the very elimination of what we all know to exist (e.g., beliefs) or the reduction to deterministic biochemical processes of what we all know to be free (e.g., thoughts, the will), still the only explanations considered acceptable for discussion, the only explanations conceivable, the only explanations to be in any manner entertained by rational minds are — you guessed it — natural explanations.

Even as his approach to the world reduces human reasoning itself to absurdity, the naturalist scientist will patiently explain to us that Christian theism isn't reasonable, and that the rational man can only accept a mind reduced to deterministic physical processes, devoid of reason.

It's enough to make a man *wish* he were insane.

(On second thought, a scientist who posits the possibility that fairies are responsible for fall foliage is not that far removed from Richard Dawkins' fantastic theorizing that life on earth could possibly be explained by space aliens "seeding" this planet, long ago . . . is he?)

BUT ISN'T THIS ALL A CIRCULAR ARGUMENT? AFTER ALL, GOD'S EXISTENCE IS THE VERY POINT IN QUESTION!

This is a strange objection to make in light of its converse: the question-begging assumption of the truth of naturalism as the *basis* for scientific arguments against God.

But that aside, it is simply not the case that we have argued in a circle or begged the question in this book. Theists don't say, "God exists; therefore God exists." Therefore, neither is our argument circular. If anything it's been structured thus:

> A law of morality exists and is known to all — and therefore, God exists. Consciousness exists, and the mind; reason, and the laws of logic; human worth, dignity, and equal rights; free will, human

personality, love, purpose, and meaning — and therefore, God exists.

In short, we assert that the very notions of *possibility and impossibility* require God's existence; that, in fact, it is impossible that God *not* exist.

The debate over the existence of God allows only two possibilities. Either God exists or he doesn't. There is no middle ground.[118] Our argument is that if it can be conclusively demonstrated that the logical conclusions entailed by an atheist-naturalist position are absurd, inconsistent with reality, and, therefore, impossible in practice, then atheism is shown to be false — and, therefore, God must exist.

To illustrate this last point, think once more about Richard Dawkins and Christopher Hitchens. In order to speak, write, and argue their naturalistic case, they first need to formulate the case. This entails the development of thoughts and ideas, the use of reason, and the application of the laws of logic. That, in turn, means that Dawkins and Hitchens must assume the essential reliability of human reasoning as a means of coming to the truth of how things are in the real world outside their brains. But this then means that they must backtrack to demonstrate how a naturalist viewpoint can account for even the existence of the mind *before* they can assume any essential reliability of human reasoning as a means of coming to the truth . . .

Which they can't.

Interestingly enough, it isn't Christian theists who toss up "*mental* roadblocks" in the path of atheists like

Richard Dawkins and Christopher Hitchens as they try to paint themselves as barreling down the eight-lane superhighway of Reason — it's their fellow atheists. Other naturalist scientists and philosophers *themselves* are the ones continually reminding these men that their ideas are nothing but the result of electro-chemical processes in their brains. They're the ones insisting that the universe is "matter and matter only." And they have, therefore, denied the existence of the *immaterial mind* (as opposed to the organic brain matter in their heads) as well as the *transcendent laws of reason and logic* (which they know are not the same thing as electro-chemical reactions in their brains).

Never mind the non-existence of God; naturalistic atheism cannot produce what is needed to make a case for *anything* — and as such, is a viciously self-refuting proposition. In the end, Dawkins and Hitchens and their colleagues not only are nowhere near the on-ramp to this great superhighway of Science and Reason; they can't even get their cars started.

> Never mind the non-existence of God; naturalistic atheism cannot produce what is needed to make a case for *anything* — and as such, is a viciously self-refuting proposition.

THE (INCONVENIENT) RECALCITRANT FACT

In short, our argument for the existence of God is far from "circular." In this book, we have merely proposed to consider naturalism as a theory and test its claims to see if the theory is valid. This method should certainly not seem strange to the modern scientific mind; scientists think in terms of "explanatory hypotheses" all the time.

Let's consider an example drawn from chemistry. Suppose that scientists know that such-and-such a colorless chemical, when applied to metal and then exposed to high heat, will turn bright red. Next, someone tells you that this bottle on the table contains that chemical; he applies several drops of the liquid to a spoon and holds it over a flame, but the liquid doesn't turn red. In fact, it doesn't change color at all. This is evidence that what you were told about that particular chemical is false. There may be other possible explanations for why the liquid did not turn bright red, but certainly one of those possibilities is that the liquid used was not the chemical in question. Thus develops an explanatory hypothesis.

Scientists test explanatory hypotheses by their ability to account for the facts. Someone insists that the world is made of water (as the Greek philosopher Thales did), and scientists can test the idea. When one of them discovers that there exist certain elements that are not water and are not reducible to water, the every-thing-is-water hypothesis will be abandoned. This is how science works: a theory is proposed and tested to see if it will account for all facts involved.

Now, a false theory may explain some of the facts quite nicely, but then it faces what is known as a "recalcitrant fact." J. P. Moreland explains that term:

> . . . a fact that is obstinate, uncooperative, a fact that doggedly resists explanation by a theory. No matter what a theory's advocate does, the recalcitrant fact

just sits there and is not easily incorporated into the theory. In this case, the recalcitrant fact provides falsifying evidence for the theory.[119]

In the case of the naturalist theory, we contend that the existence of the human person himself — complete with immaterial qualities and faculties that are not reducible to matter — serves as an insurmountable recalcitrant fact that, by itself, demonstrates that the naturalist theory is irretrievably false.

What your experience as a human being tells you is *true*, an atheist is forced to deny, seek to eliminate, or find some explanation of. He will have no choice but to try to convince you that what you *know* exists doesn't really exist, at least not in any immaterial sense: it's all consequences of certain minute electro-chemical emissions coursing through your brain. Free will is an illusion; your thoughts, dreams, and plans for the future are nothing more than peculiar confluences of "particles and their relations," a "vast assemblage of nerve cells and their associated molecules."

Honestly. This type of grasping-at-straws in an effort to avoid, at all costs, the looming possibility of God's existence is no more "scientific" than Richard Dawkins' deer-in-the-headlights theory that space aliens might have "seeded" life on earth.

The atheist becomes, inevitably, like a man who packs for a trip with a suitcase that's far too small for everything he tries to put in it. And so, shirtsleeves, socks, bits of trouser cuffs, neckties, and underwear hang out from every side of the bulging container. At the airport, the airline agent behind the ticket counter stops him.

"Sir," she says, "you have a lot of items hanging outside your suitcase, and we don't allow that. If you want to check that suitcase, you will need to find some way to fit everything inside it."

How does the man respond? By taking a pair of scissors and cutting away everything hanging outside the suitcase — in the process, completely ruining all the clothes inside. Yet once finished, he cheerfully tells the agent, "No problem. As you can see, everything fits now."

Just so, the only way for atheism to explain man is, in effect, to abolish man.

By contrast, the moment one assumes the existence of God and the possibility that God created man in His own image, everything we actually *see* and know to be true about human beings immediately makes sense. There is no need to deny, eliminate, reduce, or explain away anything.

"Swinging a Wide Rope"

Now let's consider what may be the classic objection to the argument against the atheist worldview, frequently expressed as follows:

> Your argument for God's existence seems to be that, without God, atheists can't have morals or reason, that they can't believe in rights or in the reality of love or that life has meaning. It is perfectly obvious, however, that atheists do indeed have all of these things without believing in God. Most atheists are some of the nicest, most moral people around, and some are far more reasonable and tolerant than many

who believe in God. Atheists uphold the dignity of human persons and champion human rights all over the world. Atheists fall in love, get married, cherish their children, and love their family and friends as much as anyone else, certainly as much as any theist does. Don't these facts demonstrate that your anti-naturalist argument is really nothing but a straw-man caricature of atheism, that it doesn't represent atheists or atheism as they really are?

First, while we can for the most part agree with what is said here about atheists as *individuals*, what's said about the *argument* we present is erroneous.

We freely admit that most atheists are moral, decent men and women whose lives include love, friendship, and the like. We've emphasized that a number of times in this book. Our argument has never been that atheists "can't have morals or reason or value." Our argument has been that atheists cannot *account* for morality, reason, or value *on the basis of the worldview they insist to be true*.

In this, we assert that the atheist worldview is like that of the man mentioned at the beginning of this book who denies the existence of gravity. He proclaims his conviction that gravity does not exist — while in the real world, every step he takes proves him wrong. Regardless of how strenuously he may protest to the contrary, he simply cannot escape the *reality* of gravity. What he *says* and what he has no choice but to *do* are diametrically opposed.

This is the predicament of the Godless delusion.

> Our argument has never been that atheists "can't" have morals or reason or value." Our argument has been that atheists cannot *account* for morality, reason, or value *on the basis of the worldview they insist to be true.*

The atheist is, in fact, living on borrowed capital. Specifically, he's living on capital borrowed from the Christian theistic worldview — declaring confidently that God cannot exist, while making full use of all those good things that God's existence makes possible.

In this, he's much like the cattle rustler of the Old West. The typical cattle rustler had corrals full of cattle and made a good income. In all externals, he appeared to be just another legitimate rancher. The difference was that the legitimate rancher could account for his cattle. The rustler couldn't. The legitimate cattle rancher could explain how and when those cows came into his possession — bills of sale, transaction records, etc. The cattle rustler couldn't. Most or all of "his" cattle were those he stole from legitimate ranchers.

Analogously, the atheist's "corral" is filled with his own morals, knowledge, human value, dignity, love, rights, self-awareness, meaning, free will, appreciation for beauty, respect for ideas, and hunger for what will make him truly happy. Many fine head of cattle, indeed! And he lives each day as though each of these good things belonged to him — which, ironically, they do, as he belongs to God and is created in the very image of God.

But, like the rustler, the atheist's worldview cannot account for *how he came to possess* these good things. The atheist cattle rustler has been "swinging a wide rope," as they used to say derisively about cattle thieves in the Old West. He has, in fact, "borrowed" his cattle from a worldview that *can* account for them.

It's worth saying as well that the presuppositional argument presented in this book is not, in any sense, an attack on atheists as *persons*. Rather, it's a challenge to them to rethink — and, hopefully, abandon — their naturalist worldview. Even with the "cattle rustling," naturalists are just doing what they have to do as they attempt to live in God's world, yet convince themselves at the same time that God doesn't even exist.

Our basic metaphorical question to the atheist-cattle-rustler is, "How'd you get them cattle?" He doesn't owe us an answer, but he does owe himself one. A good one, not the gobbledygook pseudo-scientific feel-good answer that naturalism promises but can never deliver in any coherently true manner.

Our desire is to lead those who are — deliberately or unwittingly — ensnared in the Godless delusion to recognize that their position is bankrupt. We want to help them see that a good and loving God really does exist, and that all human beings, including every last atheist who walks the face of the earth, has been created in the image of that living God.

Apologetics is the mission of assisting those we love back to sanity. We want to help them see that their natural desires for purpose and meaning, their natural intuitions about right and wrong and value and knowledge, have from the beginning been pointing them in the right direction.

CHANGE THE IDEA, CHANGE THE WORLD

"Ideas," Auguste Comte once said, "make the world or throw it into chaos."

A civilization in which children are taught that they are nothing more than complex material beings — who have ultimately come from nowhere and are ultimately going nowhere — cannot result in a happy, healthy civilization.

A society in which children are encouraged, "Do the right thing, but remember that right and wrong don't exist and are up to you to define," cannot produce better and higher morals.

An educational system that insists that "the brain is governed solely by the laws of chemistry and physics"[120] and therefore that "you" — your sense of personal identity and free will — are, in fact, no more than the behavior of a "vast assembly of nerve cells" cannot result in anything but hopelessness regarding morality, knowledge, and meaning.

At some point, the implications of naturalism — that system through which modern man understands himself — will become clear. Everyone will know that nothing can be known. Then, the individual pursuit of money, power, and pleasure can truly take its place at the center of everything.

Or . . . there may be a return to a worldview that can make sense of our lives.

The day is coming. But it will take time for modern secular man to fully see the implications of the freedoms he's giving away and the chains of slavery he has embraced.

WHAT NEXT?

In conclusion, atheists should ask themselves a few hard questions that require honest answers:

- What if naturalism is *not* true?
- What if the universe we live in is the one that Christian theists say God created?
- What if God really does exist?
- What then?

Intellectually honest atheists will not ignore the challenge proffered in this book: Don't just consider the possibility that God might exist, but confront the evidence we have presented here and reckon with the *necessity* of his existence. Grapple with the numerous and compelling philosophical, cosmological, and commonsense arguments in favor of theism that must be allowed into the discussion. Ignoring these, ultimately, is the philosophical equivalent of engaging in junk science.

No honest scientist worth his grant money excludes potentially contradictory scientific evidence from his experiments simply because he wants to ensure his desired outcome in his findings. That would constitute scientific fraud, and any scientist who fudged the facts that way, or simply ignored inconvenient evidence, would quickly become a pariah in the scientific community. His scientific "findings," in any case, would be worthless because he intentionally ignored valid, relevant evidence. That kind of "science" amounts to little more than a stuffed ballot box in a rigged election.

The Christian philosophical case for God's existence is formidable, compelling, and not in the least unwilling to take on the best and brightest apologists for atheism and deal with their arguments. After reading this book, we encourage all intellectually honest atheists and skeptics to take the next step and confront the case for God, presented in works such as:

- *The Last Superstition: A Refutation of Modern Atheism* (Edward Feser)
- *Handbook of Christian Apologetics* (Peter Kreeft and Ronald Tacelli)
- *The One and the Many* (Peter Kreeft and Ronald Tacelli)
- *What's So Great About Christianity?* (Dinesh D'Souza)
- *Theology and Sanity* (Frank Sheed)

The list of such good books is long, but these will get you started in the right direction.

It is the authors' sincere hope that all atheists who read this book will at least be willing to think through the implications of the position they have taken, to think them through with rigorous consistency, and to think them through (literally) to their "bitter end." We have tried to show that the inescapable rational implications of the naturalist worldview are both unthinkable and unlivable.

It makes us wonder why the Godless delusion of atheism is so attractive to so many otherwise intelligent people. Why do they fall for it?

Perhaps it's because atheist naturalism is the Big Lie that is constantly, incessantly repeated in classrooms, in the media, and around dinner tables everywhere. As Vladimir Lenin, the atheist architect of Soviet Communism, once said, "If you tell a lie big enough and keep repeating it, people will eventually come to believe it."

The "old story," as we mentioned at the beginning of his book, was the story of Christian theism. The "new story" that has now taken its place as the "official" story of modern Western civilization is the story of atheistic naturalism. But that's not because naturalism, with its inherent denial of the existence of God, has in any sense whatsoever been demonstrated to be true, or Christian theism to be false.

No, Christian theism is rejected by an increasing number of Westerners not because it has been legitimately vanquished by scientific naturalism, but merely because *it is thought to have been.* And also because — well, it's the "old story." Outdated. An old-school way that our "unenlightened" ancestors" understood the world as best they could, with their primitive superstitions hampering them from understanding scientific truth — which burst brightly

> Christian theism is rejected by an increasing number of Westerners not because it has been legitimately vanquished by scientific naturalism, but merely because *it is thought to have been.*

upon mankind with the advent of the Enlightenment.

When widespread belief in the "old story" of Christian theism began to wane and the "new story" of atheist naturalism began to gain traction, then momentum, and finally, *power*, the attitude of many atheists started to sound like dialogue from an old Western:

> "There's a new sheriff in town now, see? His name is Science. And this town ain't big enough for Science and Christianity. So, Christianity, you'd better just saddle up and ride quietly off into the sunset of yesterday — into the murky twilight of the era of myth and superstition and religion. *Adios, muchacho. Vaya con Dios.*"

But, fortunately, Christians haven't been fooled. Their comeback?

> "Not so fast, my pointy-headed, lab-coated *amigo*. Christianity has been around these parts for a very long time. Christianity has met in mortal combat, on the battlefield of reason and evidence, and has vanquished far more formidable adversaries than Richard Dawkins and his brand of 'scientific atheism.' You're right that this town ain't big enough for the two of us, but you can be darned sure that Christianity is not going anywhere. And no dandified scientific bully is going to chase it away."

The challenge of this book you've just finished reading is that, as "installed" as this new sheriff might seem to be, as authoritatively as he may seem to speak . . . he's really just shooting blanks.

ENDNOTES

1 This motto was formally adopted by a joint resolution of Congress and signed into law by President Dwight Eisenhower on July 30, 1956.

2 Hundreds of such books have been written and published in recent decades, though these are among the better known ones.

3 Cf. BBC: "UK Among Most Secular Nations," http://news.bbc.co.uk/2/hi/programmes/wtwtgod/3518375.stm; the Pew Research Center: "The 2004 Political Landscape: Religion in American Life," available at http://people-press.org/report/?pageid=757. Demographics of Atheism, http://en.wikipedia.org/wiki/Demographics_of_atheism. Numerous surveys are presented here.

4 "The Demographics of Atheism" article at http://en.wikipedia.org/wiki/Demographics_of_atheism.

5 Philip Johnson, *Reason in the Balance* (Downers Grove, IL: Intervarsity Press, 1995), p. 7-8.

6 This theme has been beautifully developed in John Eldredge's book *Epic*.

7 Theoretically, the arguments made in this book against the

atheist-naturalist worldview and for the existence of God are arguments Jews and Muslims and any other believer could make to the extent that he believes in the existence of an infinite personal God who created the world, and uniquely created mankind in His image and likeness, not some vague impersonal "force." We will use "Christian theism" to denote our position throughout this book, first for simplicity's sake (it's easier than writing six or seven times per page "Christian, Jewish and Islamic theism, as well as anyone else who believes in an infinite personal God who created the world and made man in his image and likeness," but also because Christian theism — not Jewish or Islamic — *was* in fact the accepted worldview of Western civilization until it was supplanted in our modern age by the worldview of scientific naturalism. And this is the context in which we write.

8   Johnson, *Reason in the Balance*, p. 14.

9   "Leading Scientists Still Reject God," *Nature,* vol. 394, July 23, 1998; http://www.stephenjaygould.org/ctrl/news/file002.html. Obviously, we are not here saying that God created human or animal *artifacts*: i.e., the Space Shuttle, a beaver dam, a bird's nest, and the Great Wall of China are things that exist in the cosmos but are merely artifacts created by humans and animals using pre-existing materials. But it is God who created out of nothing (Latin: *ex nihilo*) all the material of the cosmos and ordered it in such a way that it would behave and function according to the cosmic laws of nature He put in play.

10 Jesse Bering, "Science Will Never Silence God," from *The Best American Non-Required Reading,* ed. Dave Eggers (New York: Mariner Books, 2007), p. 116.

11 Emphasis added.

12 Emphasis added.

13 We are neither saying nor implying that *we* are God. The New Age actress and author, Shirley MacLaine, God bless her, was dead wrong when she proclaimed to all who would listen, "I am God! I am God!"

14 www.despair.com.

15 Paul Edwards, *The Encyclopedia of Philosophy* (New York: Macmillan Publishing Co. 1967), Vol. 5, p. 448.

16 Ibid., p. 179.

17 Ibid., p. 183.

18 C. S. Lewis, *Mere Christianity* (San Francisco: Harper Collins, 1952), p. 3.

19 Ibid., 6-7.

20 Cf. St. Thomas Aquinas, *Summa Theologiae*, I, Q. 6, a. 1-4.

21 Ibid., Q. 17, art. 3; Q. 79, art. 11; Q. 83, art. 3; Q. 84.

22 *De veritate* (*On Truth*), Q. 1, art. 9; *De potentia Dei* (*On the Power of God*) Q. 3, art. 15.

23 Catholic philosopher Norris Clarke, S. J., adds some additional precision to our discussion here of what it means for something to exist: "Being = that which is. When used without qualification = a real being = that which actually exists with its own act of existence outside of an idea. When specified as a *mental being* = that which is present not by its own act of existence but only inside an idea. Its being is its to-be-thought-about." *The One*

and the Many: A Contemporary Thomistic Metaphysics (Notre Dame: University of Notre Dame Press, 2001), 316; cf. pp. 25-91.

24 J. P. Moreland and Kai Nielsen, *Does God Exist?* (Amherst: Prometheus Books, 1993), p. 113.

25 The *Encyclopedia Britannica* defines this kind of relativism as a philosophical view that what is right or wrong and good or bad is not absolute but variable and relative, depending on the person, circumstances, or social situation. . . . Because what people think will vary with time and place, what is right will also vary. If, however, changing and even conflicting moral principles are equally valid, there is apparently no objective way of justifying any principle as valid for all people and all societies.

26 Charles Templeton, *Farewell to God: My Reasons for Rejecting the Christian Faith* (Toronto: McClelland & Stuart, 1996), p. 205.

27 J. L. Mackie, *The Miracle of Theism* (Oxford: Clarendon Press, 1982), p. 115.

28 Moreland and Nielsen, p. 114.

29 Quoted by Ravi Zacharias, *Can Man Live Without God* (Dallas: Word Publishing, 1994), p. 28.

30 Dinesh D'Souza, *Was Hitler a Christian? Dinesh D'Souza Blog* (November 1, 2007). D'Souza continues:

Hitler's *Table Talk*, a revealing collection of the Fuhrer's private opinions, assembled by a close aide during the war years, shows Hitler to be rabidly anti-religious. He called Christianity one of the great "scourges" of history, and said of the Germans, "Let's be the only people who are immunized against this disease." He promised that "through the peasantry we shall be able to destroy Christianity." In fact, he blamed the Jews for inventing Christianity. He also condemned Christianity for its opposition to evolution. Hitler reserved special scorn for the Christian values of equality and compassion, which he identified with weakness. Hitler's leading advisers like Goebbels, Himmler, Heydrich, and Bormann were atheists who hated religion and sought to eradicate its influence in Germany. . . . Historian Allan Bullock writes that Hitler "had no time at all for Catholic teaching, regarding it as a religion fit only for slaves and detesting its ethics."

31 Quoted in *Nietzsche, Godfather of Fascism?* Edited by Jacob Golomb and Robert Wistrich (Princeton: Princeton University Press, 2002).

32 Ravi Zacharias, *Can Man Live Without God?* (Dallas: Word Publishing, 1994), p. 23.

33 Viktor Frankl, *The Doctor and the Soul: Introduction to Logotherapy* (New York: Knopf, 1982), p. xxi.

34 Auguste Comte, *Course of Positive Philosophy* (1830), from *Auguste Comte and Positivism: The Essential Writings,* edited by Gertrude Lenzer, (New York: Harper and Row, 1975), p. 83.

35 Edvard Radzinsky, *Stalin* (New York: Anchor Books, 1996), p. 155.

36 Ibid., pp. 245-247.

37 Ibid., p. 143.

38 Jung Chang and Jon Halliday, *Mao: The Unknown Story* (New York: Anchor Books, 2006), p. 3.

39 See Richard Dawkins, *The God Delusion* (Boston: Houghton Mifflin, 2006), p. 108.

40 All things, incidentally, that have been routinely perpetrated by committed atheists such as Stalin and Mao. At least they were being consistent with their heinous ideology. Atheists in general, though, seldom are consistent on this point of good and evil.

41 Modern atheist author Robert Buckman argues along these lines in his book *Can We Be Good Without God?*, as does Greg Epstein in *Good Without God: What a Billion Non-Religious People Do Believe* and Richard Dawkins does in *The God Delusion* (especially pp. 214-233).

42 Wesley J. Smith, letter, *First Things,* May 2002 at http://www.firstthings.com/article/2007/01/who-is-a-jew-38.

43 Benjamin J. Wiker, "Darwin and the Descent of Morality," *First Things,* November 2001.

44 Whom the progenitors of atheistic Communism, Karl Marx and Frederick Engels, routinely referred to as "the masses" (cf. *Manifesto of the Communist Party*).

45 We say "so-called" because a great deal of what passes for "medical ethics" within the modern Western medical establishment is anything but ethical! For an exhaustive survey of how chillingly unethical many modern medical ethicists are, see Wesley J. Smith, *The Culture of Death: The Assault on Medical Ethics in America* (Encounter Books, 2002) and *Forced Exit: Euthanasia, Assisted*

Suicide, and the New Duty to Die (Encounter Books, 2005).

46 Who, in 1953, with fellow scientist Francis Crick, discovered the double-helix construction of DNA.

47 Emphasis added.

48 Atheist standard-bearer Richard Dawkins says as much in *The God Delusion.*

49 Moreland and Nielsen, *Does God Exist?,* p. 99.

50 Ibid., p. 106.

51 Ibid., pp. 106-107.

52 Peter Kreeft and Ronald K. Tacelli, S.J., *Handbook of Christian Apologetics* (Downers Grove: InterVarsity Press, 1994), pp. 72-73.

53 Emmanuel Kant, *Critique of Pure Reason* (New York: MacMillan and Co., 1896), pp. 664-665.

54 Moreland and Nielsen, p.117.

55 Zacharias, pp. 39-40.

56 F. J. Sheed, *The Church and I* (Garden City, NY: Doubleday, 1974), p. 53.

57 Paul Churchland, *Matter and Consciousness* (Cambridge, MA: MIT Press, 1984), p. 21.

58 Francis Crick, *The Astonishing Hypothesis: The Scientific Search for the Soul* (New York: Scribners, 1995), p. 3.

59 Pierre Jean George Cabanis, *Rapport du physique et du moral de l'homme, in Oeuvres completes de Cabanis* (Paris: Bossange Freres, 1824), 3:159-60, quoted by Stanley L. Jaki, *Angels, Apes, & Men* (Peru, Illinois:

Sherwood Sugden & Company Publishers), p. 45.

60 Johnson, *Reason in the Balance*, p. 64.

61   Ibid., p. 65.

62 Peter Kreeft, *Socratic Logic* (South Bend: St. Augustine's Press, 2004), pp. 1-2, emphasis added.

63 For an excellent introduction to these common logical fallacies see Patrick J. Hurley, *A Concise Introduction to Logic* (Belmont, CA: Wadsworth Publishing Co., 1994), pp. 113-191.

64 "[E]very argument makes two basic claims: a claim that evidence exists and a claim that the alleged evidence supports something (or that something follows from the alleged evidence). The first is a factual claim, the second is an inferential claim. The evaluation of every argument centers on the evaluation of these two claims. The most important of the two is the inferential claim, because if the premises fail to support the conclusion (that is, if the reasoning is bad), an argument is worthless). Thus, we will always test the inferential claim first, and only if the premises do support the conclusion will we test the factual claim (that is, the claim that the premises present genuine evidence or are true). Hurley, pp. 41-42.

65 Some modern atheists propound the idea of "eliminative materialism," which Catholic philosopher Dr. Edward Feser describes as "an attempt to eliminate from our conception of the world everything that is essential to mind and to replace it with a materialistic-cum-mechanistic substitute. A 'materialist explanation of the mind' is this like a 'secularist explanation of God' or a 'mechanistic explanation of formal and final causes.' Secularism doesn't 'explain' God, but denies that He exists; mechanism doesn't 'explain formal and final causes,' but denies that they exist; and materialism ultimately doesn't 'explain' the mind at all, but implicitly denies that it exists.'Eliminative materialism' makes this denial explicit rather than implicit. It is sometimes characterized as an 'extreme' form of materialism, but it is more accurately described as an 'honest' or 'consistent' form of materialism. It is also insane, and a *reductio ad absurdum* of the entire materialist project" (Edward Feser, *The Last Superstition: A Refutation of the New Atheism* [South Bend: St. Augustine's Press, 2008]), p. 195.

66 Churchland, p. 21.

67 Johnson, *Reason in the Balance*, pp. 125, 128.

68 J. B. S. Haldane, *Possible Worlds*, 1927, p. 209, quoted by C. S. Lewis, *Miracles*, p. 15.

69 Stephen Hawking, *A Briefer History of Time: From the Big Bang to Black Holes* (Bantam, 1988) quoted by Johnson, p. 61.

70 Johnson, p. 62.

71 Greg L. Bahnsen, in a taped lecture on apologetics.

72 See: LifeSiteNews.com, "Planned Parenthood Nurse Admits Infanticide: 'It Does Happen'" (http://www.lifesitenews.com/ldn/2008/oct/08103101.html).

73 Wesley J. Smith describes in his books *Forced Exit: Euthanasia, Assisted Suicide, and the New Duty to Die* and *Culture of Death: The Assault on Medical Ethics in*

America how what is currently known as the "right to die" movement is morphing into what will soon become the "obligation to die" mandate — courtesy of the atheism's naturalist ideology, which is propelling the West deeper into a new moral Dark Age.

74 They boast that naturalism's "[T]riumphant progress in the twentieth century of a materialist biology and biochemistry has almost completely eliminated . . . supernatural views of life . . . repudiating the view that there exists or could exist any entities or events which lie, in principle, beyond the scope of scientific explanation." Paul Edwards, editor, *The Encyclopedia of Philosophy* (New York: Macmillan Publishing Co., 1967), vol. 5, pp. 183, 448.

75 W. T. Jones, *A History of Western Philosophy* (New York: Harcourt, Brace and Co., 1952), p. 528.

76 Michael Ruse, "Evolutionary Theory and Christian Ethics," in *The Darwinian Paradigm* (London: Routledge, 1989), pp. 262-269.

77 George Gaylord Simpson, *The Meaning of Evolution* (New Haven, CT: Yale University Press, 1967), p. 345.

78 Douglas Futuyma, *Science on Trial: The Case for Evolution* (Pantheon, 1983), pp. 12-13, quoted in Johnson, p. 9.

79 J. P. Moreland, *The Recalcitrant* Imago Dei: *Human Persons and the Failure of Naturalism* (London, UK: SCM Press, 2009), pp. 144-145.

80 Edward N. Barlow, *The Autobiography of Charles Darwin* (New York: Harcourt Brace, 1959), p. 92 (emphasis added).

81 Ibid.

82 James Rachels, *Created from Animals* (Oxford: Oxford University Press, 1990), pp. 171-172.

83 *Vogue* Magazine, September 1, 1989.

84 *Washingtonian* Magazine, February 1, 1990.

85 Richard Dawkins, *River out of Eden: A Darwinian View of Life* (London: Phoenix, 1995), p. 133.

86 James Rachels, *Created from Animals*, p. 70.

87 By the way, this atheist attempt to defend human dignity also fails because each of the qualities listed as criteria by which one could be said to possess "value" exists in gradation. Not everyone loves and is loved at the same level. Not everyone creates at the same level. Not everyone contributes to society at the same level. Not everyone has the same talents and abilities. In which case, we would have to conclude that some possess more value than others.

88 The National Institute of Mental Health reports: "In 2006, suicide was the third leading cause of death for young people ages 15 to 24" (http://www.nimh.nih.gov/health/publications/suicide-in-the-us-statistics-and-prevention/index.shtml).

89 Christopher Hitchens and Rabbi Schmuley Boteach Debate on God's Existence, January 30, 2008, at the 92nd St. Y in New York. available digitally at http://www.youtube.com/watch?v=vnMYL8sF7bQ.

90 Cf. Written in French (*"Je pense donc je suis"*) in *Discourse on the Method* part IV (1637), and in Latin in *Principles of Philosophy* part I, art. 7 (1644).

91 Geoffrey Madell, *Mind and Materialism* (Edinburgh: Edinburgh University Press, 1988), p. 141.

92 Colin McGinn, *The Mysterious Flame* (New York: Basic Books, 1999), pp. 13-14.

93 Jaegwon Kim, *Philosophy of Mind* (Boulder, CO: Westview, 1996), p. 8, quoted ibid, p. 36.

94 Moreland, *The Recalcitrant* Imago Dei, p. 17.

95 The video of this exchange between Stein and Dawkins can be seen online at http://www.youtube.com/watch?v=GlZtEjtlirc.

96 George Wald, a chemistry professor at Harvard University, expressed pretty clearly the naturalist conception of human personality when he said, "400 years ago there was a collection of molecules named Shakespeare, which produced Hamlet." Quoted in Francis A. Schaeffer, *How Should We Then Live? The Rise and Decline of Western Thought and Culture* (Old Tappan, NJ: Fleming H. Revell Company), p.164.

97 In *Why We Love: the Nature and Chemistry of Romantic Love,* Helen Fisher says that human love can largely be explained by the effect the chemicals dopamine and norepinephrine have on the brain.

98 Patrick Madrid, "Conclusions of a Guilty Bystander," in *Surprised by Truth 2* (Manchester, NH: Sophia Institute Press, 2000), pp. 171-172.

99 Listen to Joaquín Rodriguez's *Concierto de Aranjuez* or Maurice Ravel's *Pavane for a Dead Princess* and see what power such exquisite music can have to move your soul.

100 See Dinesh D'Souza's refutation of the atheist denial of an afterlife in *Life After Death: The Evidence* (Washington, DC: Regnery Press, 2010).

101 Referring here to the Quecreek Mine Rescue of the miners trapped due to a flooded mine shaft in July of 2002. See Chapter Seven.

102 John Searle, *Freedom and Neurobiology* (New York: Columbia University Press, 2007), cited by Moreland, *The Recalcitrant* Imago Dei, p. 41.

103 John Searle, *Minds, Brains and Science* (Cambridge, MA: Harvard University Press, 2000), pp. 86-87.

104 From the Greek *telos*, meaning "end" or "purpose."

105 Edward Feser, *The Last Superstition: A Refutation of the New Atheism* (South Bend: St. Augustine's Press, 2008), p. 36.

106 Cf. *The Baltimore Catechism*, question 150.

107 Bertrand Russell, *A Free Man's Worship* (1903). http://www.philosophicalsociety.com/Archives/A%20 Free%20Man%27s%20Worship.htm.

108 Cited in Clark Pinnock, *Are There Any Answers?* (Minneapolis: Dimension Books, 1976) p. 14.

109 Stephen Jay Gould, "The Meaning of Life," in *LIFE* magazine (December 1988), p. 84; quoted by Moreland, *The Recalcitrant* Imago Dei, p. 51.

110 Jones, *A History of Western Philosophy*, p. 530.

111 Friedrich Nietzsche, *The Parable of the Madman,* from *Primary Source Readings in World Religions*, editor Jeffrey Brodd (Winona, MN: Saint Mary's Press, 2009), pp. 229-230.

112 John Searle, *Freedom and Neurobiology: Reflections on Free Will, Language and Political Power* (New York: Columbia University Press, 2007), pp. 4, 5.

113 Dallas Willard, "Knowledge and Naturalism" in *Naturalism: A Critical Analysis*, edited by William Lane Craig and J. P. Moreland (London: Routledge, 2000), 51 pp. Available digitally at: http://www.dwillard.org/articles/artview.asp?artID=64.

114 See W. Norris Clarke, S.J., for a summary of the primary defects in the Humeian and Kantian alternatives to metaphysics, *The One and the Many: A Modern Thomistic Metaphysics* (South Bend: University of Notre Dame Press, 2001), 8-14, 37-41, 124-130.

115 John Searle, *The Rediscovery of the Mind* (Cambridge, MA: The MIT Press, 1992), p. 85, quoted in Willard, "Knowledge and Naturalism."

116 Many in the scientific community adhere to "physicalism," which is a particular version of the naturalist worldview. The *Stanford Encyclopedia of Philosophy* defines it thusly:

> Physicalism is the thesis that everything is physical, or as contemporary philosophers sometimes put it, that everything supervenes on, or is necessitated by, the physical. The thesis is usually intended as a metaphysical thesis, parallel to the thesis attributed to the ancient Greek philosopher Thales, that everything is water, or the idealism of the eighteenth-century philosopher Berkeley, that everything is mental. The general idea is that the nature of the actual world (i.e., the universe and everything in it)

conforms to a certain condition, the condition of being physical. Of course, physicalists don't deny that the world might contain many items that at first glance don't seem physical — items of a biological, or psychological, or moral, or social nature. But they insist nevertheless that at the end of the day, such items are either physical or supervene on the physical (http://plato.stanford.edu/entries/physicalism).

117 Those who don't remember the '80s can watch the video here: http://www.youtube.com/watch?v=V83JR2IoI8k.

118 This is known in philosophy as the principle of the excluded middle.

119 Moreland, *The Recalcitrant* Imago Dei, p. 4.

120 Leda Cosmides and John Tooby, *Evolutionary Psychology: A Primer* (1998), available at www.psych.uscb.edu/research/cep/primer.html.

INDEX

———◆◉◆———

About the Authors

————⊶❁⊷————

PATRICK MADRID is a lifelong Catholic who holds a B.Phil. in philosophy and is completing an MA in theology. He is the director of the Envoy Institute of Belmont Abbey College (envoyinstitute.net) and the host of the Thursday edition of EWTN's "Open Line" radio broadcast. He and his wife, Nancy, and their children live in central Ohio. His Web site is patrickmadrid.com.

KENNETH HENSLEY holds a master's degree from Fuller Theological Seminary. A respected Catholic apologist and teacher, he appears on EWTN and speaks at conferences across the country on Catholic and Protestant history and theology, as well as theistic apologetics. He resides in the Los Angeles area with his wife, Tina.